# Beth Russell's
# WILLIAM MORRIS
# NEEDLEPOINT

# Beth Russell's
# WILLIAM MORRIS
# NEEDLEPOINT

Special photography by Jan Baldwin

Crown Publishers, Inc.
New York

*For my brother, Roy Haynes,*
*in memory of our parents*

Published by Crown Publishers, Inc., 201 East 50th Street, New York, New York 10022.
Member of the Crown Publishing Group.

CROWN is a trademark of Crown Publishers, Inc.

Originally published in Great Britain by
Conran Octopus Limited in 1995

Library of Congress Cataloging in Publication Data is available upon request

ISBN 0-517-70166-9
10 9 8 7 6 5 4 3 2

*Art editor:* Leslie Harrington
*Project editor:* Helen Ridge
*Chart illustrator:* Ethan Danielson
*Picture researcher:* Claire Taylor
*Production:* Jill Macey
*Stylist:* Cathy Sinker

Printed in China

# CONTENTS

# FOREWORD

*What business have we with art at all,*
*unless we can share it.*

IT IS SURPRISINGLY difficult to pinpoint Morris's greatness. Designer, weaver, writer, dyer, lecturer – to excel at just one would have been impressive enough, but it is the sheer scale of his achievements that makes Morris truly great. Nonetheless, he provides inspiration and encouragement; the creative process was for him, as it is for us, a challenge as well as a reward.

Through all Morris's many talents runs a thread, which for me is unique. He is a weaver of dreams. He weaves them into his tapestries and draws them into his designs. They take us out of ourselves and into the safe world of gentle colors, soft lines, and interesting complexity. His poems and romances, with their mythical people in dreamlike landscapes, teach us not historical facts but a way of life, morality, and how to lose ourselves in a well-told tale.

As all stitchers know, when we pick up a needle we pick up, too, the threads of the dreams we had put down the last time we stitched; and so it is with all creative pursuits. This is partly what Morris wanted us to experience – the trials and joys of creation and the peace we can experience in the process.

Many of us, I know, find tranquility in the quiet stitching of a prescribed design in predetermined colors. Morris would have urged us to use the design as inspiration. He would have suggested that we take his designs as a starting point to strive to produce our own versions, to test ourselves and our creative ability and, indeed, find ourselves. I hope that through this book you will find the courage to explore new fabrics, threads, and ideas – and the peace of dreams.

William Morris has become so much a part of my daily life that it is easy to imagine that I knew him. My childhood is a jumble of happy memories of wood shavings, oil paints, and French polish as my father strove to master a new skill. Like Morris, my father was never content until he thoroughly understood the process of creating. Recently, I read a letter that Morris wrote to his dye specialist, Thomas Wardle, in 1877, which echoes something of what I feel about my own work: "I suspect you scarcely understand what a difficult matter it is to translate a painter's design into material. I have been at it 16 years and have never quite succeeded." I find this most heartening!

In my efforts to draw a thumbnail picture of William Morris, I am anxious to show not just some of his work but a little of the kind, expansive, determined, farseeing character that I have admired most of my life. If you glean only a little of his enthusiasm for art, practiced "by the people and for the people," and a little of his confidence to learn and experiment, then I will not have totally failed. Our best motto is the one that Morris adopted for his own – "IF I CAN."

THIS PORTRAIT BY G. F. WATTS WAS PAINTED WHEN MORRIS WAS 46. WHEN I LOOK AT IT, I AM REMINDED OF WHAT THE HISTORIAN E. P. THOMPSON SAID OF MORRIS: "HE IS ONE OF THOSE MEN WHOM HISTORY WILL NEVER OVERTAKE."

# INTO THE FOREST

𝔉air now is the springtide, now earth lies beholding

𝔚ith the eyes of a lover, the face of the sun

𝔏ong lasteth the daylight and hope is enfolding

𝔗he green growing acres with increase begun

*The Message of the March Wind*, 1886

*La Belle Dame sans Merci*, PAINTED BY JOHN WILLIAM WATERHOUSE IN 1893. THIS PAINTING IS SO ROMANTIC THAT IT COULD HAVE BEEN AN ILLUSTRATION FOR ONE OF MORRIS'S OWN BOOKS. EVERYTHING ABOUT IT – THE PERFECT BEAUTY, THE GALLANT KNIGHT, THE STREAM GLIMPSED THROUGH THE FORBIDDING WOOD, EVEN THE WILD FLOWERS – CONJURES UP A TYPICAL MORRIS DREAM.

AFTER WILLIAM MORRIS'S DEATH in 1896, his best friend was heard to muse that Morris "was born knowing most things." Indeed, it must have seemed so, for during a comparatively short life he was to show a stunning range of talents.

Morris was an exceptionally gifted child, born into a wealthy family living on the edge of Epping Forest. Delving into his childhood, it is fascinating to see the tiny shoots that were the beginnings of a forest of knowledge. His medieval romanticism was formed by reading the entire works of Sir Walter Scott before the age of seven. On his pony, he explored the forest so thoroughly that he knew it "yard by yard from Wanstead to Theydon and from Hale End to Fairlop Oak." We find similarly quaint names in much of Morris's romantic writing. In the forest he found old churches, the architectural details of which he could recall as an adult, and discovered his love of wild plants and trees. One of Morris's recollections of this time conjures up a lovely picture of a happy child: "to this day when I smell a May tree I think of going to bed in the light."

This dreamer of dreams had a springtime of life of which we all might dream. It is easy to understand why, having once enjoyed this happy state of mind, Morris should always aspire to it; and, however idealistic it might seem, he wanted everyone else to experience it. He saw no reason why labor

The beasts that be in wood and waste

should reduce the excitement, achievement, and contentment in life. So, aside from providing inspiration for his later creative work, his childhood helped lay the foundations for his socialist beliefs.

Life changed for Morris when he was thirteen. His father died and he was sent away to board at Marlborough College. I think that this was a much less happy period for Morris. He was clearly not a team man in the sporting sense of the word and intellectual loners are not best suited to incarceration in a boys' boarding school. Characteristically, he turned to the school library and the surrounding meadows, buildings, and prehistoric monuments to occupy himself. Letters to his young sister expressed his desire to return home to Epping Forest, while letters written in adulthood show him fighting for the conservation of this "very curious and characteristic wood such as can be seen nowhere else."

It was during his childhood in Epping Forest that Morris first discovered tapestry. He came upon Queen Elizabeth's Hunting Lodge where he saw a

room "hung with faded greenery." This experience triggered an everlasting fascination with medieval tapestries. Tapestry-weaving as an art form had died during the Industrial Revolution and Morris, later in life, set about reviving what he considered "the noblest of all the weaving arts." However, it was not until he had mastered the techniques that Morris & Co. started to produce tapestries commercially.

With the help of a French book dating from before the French Revolution, Morris taught himself the *Hauteloom*, or High Loom, technique on a loom set up in his bedroom at Kelmscott House, Hammersmith. This must be the most difficult weaving technique, as the weaver faces the back of the fabric and has to view his work through the warp threads in a mirror set in front of him. Morris clearly loved the work; his diary tells us that he often rose at five or six-thirty in the morning to do three or four hours before the start of his normal day. One letter from Kelmscott Manor states how he longed to return to his "dear warp and weft at Hammersmith."

In 1887 Morris designed *The Forest* tapestry for Alexander Ionides, one of his most loyal patrons. This is a staggeringly lovely work, unusually much wider (15 by 4ft/4.5 by 1.2m) than it is tall. The combination of the rolling, all-enveloping acanthus, the dignity of the remarkably realistic animals, and the daintiness of the millefleurs gives the tapestry such depth and perspective that to look at it is like reading a story of magic and mystery.

One of Morris's great strengths was to recognize ability in others and to give encouragement. He delegated with ease and generosity. Philip Webb, his close friend, frequently drew the birds and animals in Morris's designs; Webb's architectural background is evident in the fine, accurate drawings for *The Forest*. Henry Dearle was Morris's first tapestry apprentice and became the chief tapestry weaver at Merton Abbey; it was he who designed the foreground foliage for *The Forest*. It is a tribute to Morris's genius that this great, improbable piece works so astoundingly well.

# Peacock

THE PEACOCK WAS A very fashionable bird during the nineteenth century; the Victorians had a taste for the exotic and there is hardly a creature that better suits this description. An amusing story concerns the painter Whistler. In 1876, he was commissioned by Lord Leyland to advise on the decoration of a room at 49 Princes Gate, Kensington. Without Leyland's consent, he joyfully painted the walls, ceilings, and shutters with peacocks and secretly invited the press, public, and friends to view. Leyland was furious and banned Whistler from his house. The Peacock room was eventually dismantled and moved to the Freer Gallery of Art, Washington, D.C.

In 1906, Halsey Ricardo's brilliant Peacock House was built for Lord Debenham, also in London's Kensington. It contains the world's largest collection of William De Morgan tiles *in situ*, with peacocks on tiles, stonework, mosaics, and paintings.

As with most things in nature, colors and shapes flow gently into each other. This is less so with birds but the peacock exhibits a remarkable collection of patterns and colors which, when seen separately, one would hardly expect to blend together as a whole. As you can see on pages 14-15, *The Forest* tapestry has faded and I was torn between depicting my Peacock as Morris's appears now or as I feel it really had been – both options in their own ways being faithful to the original. I was also aware that Morris definitely preferred the faded colors of old medieval tapestries. After some soul-searching and very many trips to photograph the peacocks in Battersea and Holland Parks, I made up my mind about which colors I would use. It is comforting to learn that it was not an easy decision for Morris to make either. In his diary for 20th May, 1881, he wrote: "Up at 5. 3½ hours tapestry. To Grange. To Queen Square. The green for Peacock all wrong... Dined A. Ionides." Alexander Ionides, a Morris patron, was the original owner of *The Forest* tapestry.

It was with a sigh of relief that I placed the completed Peacock with the other needlepoints in the series. In spite of the intensity and variety of colors in the bird, as a stitched piece it sits well with Raven, Lion, Fox, and Hare – and dominates no more than it would in life. At first, I thought that the gleam of the neck could be achieved only by using the shine of silk or cotton threads, but the wonderful range of Appleton wool yarns and the skill of my colleague Selina Winter proved me wrong.

My Peacock was first stitched on 14 threads/in canvas which, happily, made it the perfect size for a fire screen. Some time after it was completed, I was wandering through the William Morris Gallery in Walthamstow on a gloomy, winter Sunday and stopped to admire the magnificent *Woodpecker* and *Artichoke* hangings; I envied the warmth and welcoming air they give to a room. Suddenly, I had a longing to see how my Peacock would look as a very large hanging. For days I pondered on gauges of canvas, sizes of hanging, and how to stitch it since, at that time, there was no chart of the design. Zweigart very kindly sent me the 4½ threads/in canvas, 59in (150cm) wide, which made it possible to increase the size of the hanging to 73 by 50½in (185 by 128cm). I also found a stitcher who is brilliant at copying from a stitched piece onto plain canvas. At the outset I had no idea if this would work. One of the true tests of a design is to change its size drastically, and so I eagerly awaited the outcome. To say that I was thrilled by the result is an understatement!

ABOVE DETAIL FROM A 16TH-CENTURY BOOK OF HOURS THAT BELONGED TO ANTOINE LE BON, DUC DE LORRAINE.

FAR LEFT THE GREAT HALL AT ATHELHAMPTON IS A FINE EXAMPLE OF 15TH-CENTURY DOMESTIC ARCHITECTURE. MY PEACOCK ON THE EXTRAORDINARY FIRE SCREEN LOOKS AS IF IT WERE MEANT FOR THE MEDIEVAL FIREPLACE.

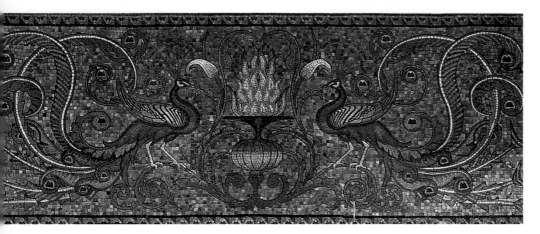

MATERIALS FOR THE PEACOCK FIRE SCREEN

**Canvas:** 14 threads/in (5.5/cm) deluxe Zweigart
   mono canvas measuring 27 x 20in (69 x 51cm)
**Threads:** Appleton crewel yarn
**Needle:** Size 20 tapestry
**Finished size of design:** 23 x 16in (58.5 x 40.5cm)
**Stitch:** Tent stitch, using 3 strands of crewel yarn

The fire screen version of the Peacock, which is charted on pages 20-3, might also be made into a large floor cushion. A cushion does, of course, need to be at least as wide as it is tall. The finished needlepoint can either be appliquéd onto the front of the cushion, or two strips of fabric can be sewn on either side. A strip of flat braid can be sewn on to help soften the joins between the fabric and the needlepoint.

The glorious Peacock wall hanging (see far right) was a total experiment; I had wanted to see how it would look as large as I could make it. It was intended to show the versatility of charts and so obviously it could not be drawn on the canvas – it had to be counted stitch for stitch and I had to be sure that the canvas was wide enough to accommodate the design. This is a simple matter of mathematics. With 228 stitches in the width of the design and 4½ stitches to each inch (1.8 stitches to each centimeter), the design takes up 50½in (128cm), so the canvas needed to be at the very least an extra 4in (10cm) in width, that is 54½in (138cm) in all.

Cross stitch is very sensible for a large piece of work as it is much less likely to distort the canvas and, of course, stretching something this large can pose some problems. Two strands of Appleton tapestry yarn cover just about well enough for a hanging, but for a piece that might need greater wearing properties, I should be inclined to use seven threads of crewel yarn on this 4½ gauge.

Due to the experimental nature of this piece, I cannot be certain about correct yarn quantities. However, the result has given me enormous pleasure and, should you wish to see a large Peacock, I urge you to try it. The size should be determined by your particular needs – where you would like to display it, how large a piece of canvas you feel you would be happy to stitch on and, indeed, the availability of the canvas. As to yarns, my advice is to buy in stages; the different dye lots one normally worries about might well be an advantage in the design and would hardly be noticed on such a fragmented background.

There are a number of very close shades in the Peacock. It would be advisable to sort and identify the colors in daylight. If they are kept in separate groups, it is much easier to select the correct threads when working in a poorer light. This is not possible for different areas of the bird, but the color numbers as they appear are:
**Head:** 465, 824, 998, 989, 488, 761, 966
**Neck:** 465, 824, 464, 488, 566
**Centre back:** 831, 526, 353, 566
**Main wing:** 186, 989, 761
**Orange underwing:** 477, 478, 765
**Breast:** 998, 465, 833, 647
**Legs:** 989, 761, 302
**Background to top of train:** 647, 356, 966
**Eyes at top of train:** 526, 765, 824, 464
**Background to bottom of train:** 356, 833, 353,
   966, 526
**Eyes at bottom of train:** 831, 765, 824, 464
Please note that the acanthus leaves are stitched in two "sets" of colors, the greener sides of the leaves with 156, 644, 642, and 641, the bluer sides with 156, 155, 154, and 521. Both sides have 156 for the veins.

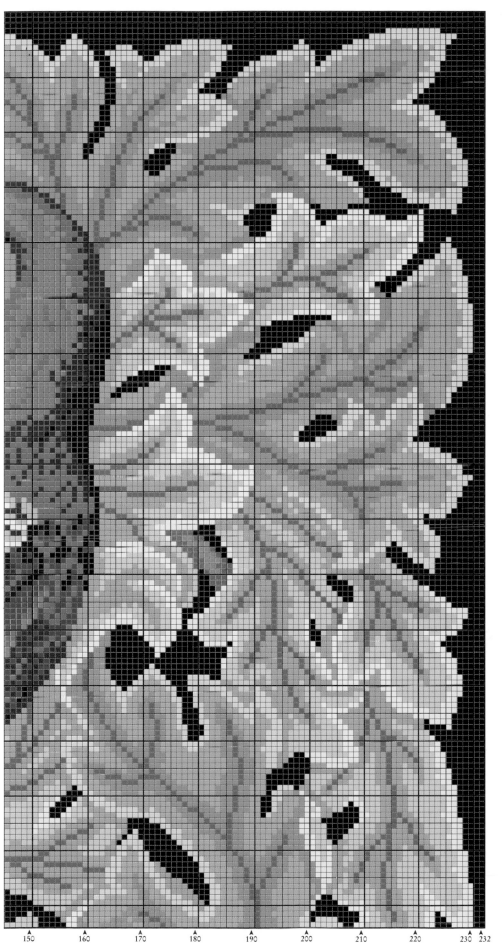

## CHART AND COLOR KEY

The Peacock fire screen was made in Appleton crewel yarn. The bottom half of the chart appears on pages 22-3.

| | | | | |
|---|---|---|---|---|
| ■ | **504** Scarlet<br>1 skein | | **642** Light blue-green<br>8 skeins |
| ■ | **204** Dusky pink<br>1 skein | | **641** Light greeny-turquoise<br>3 skeins |
| ■ | **708** Light pink<br>1 skein | | **647** Darkest green<br>2 skeins |
| ■ | **478** Dark orangey-ginger<br>1 skein | | **833** Dark jade green<br>2 skeins |
| ■ | **477** Mid orangey-ginger<br>1 skein | | **831** Light jade green<br>1 skein |
| ■ | **765** Ginger<br>2 skeins | | **156** Darkest gray-blue<br>8 skeins |
| ■ | **471** Yellow<br>1 skein | | **155** Mid gray-blue<br>8 skeins |
| □ | **872** Pastel yellow<br>1 skein | | **154** Lighter gray-blue<br>8 skeins |
| ■ | **186** Dark chocolate<br>2 skeins | | **526** Turquoise<br>1 skein |
| ■ | **913** Mid brown<br>1 skein | | **521** Light turquoise<br>3 skeins |
| ■ | **302** Light pinky-brown<br>1 skein | | **566** Marine blue<br>1 skein |
| ■ | **761** Light fawn<br>1 skein | | **488** Bright kingfisher<br>1 skein |
| ■ | **356** Darkest leaf green<br>3 skeins | | **465** Very dark royal blue<br>1 skein |
| ■ | **355** Green<br>1 skein | | **824** Dark royal blue<br>1 skein |
| ■ | **354** Mid green<br>3 skeins | | **464** Mid royal blue<br>2 skeins |
| ■ | **353** Light leaf green<br>1 skein | | **998** Charcoal<br>1 skein |
| ■ | **352** Lightest green<br>3 skeins | | **966** Dark gray<br>1 skein |
| ■ | **293** Gray-green<br>2 skeins | | **989** Light gray<br>1 skein |
| ■ | **644** Mid blue-green<br>8 skeins | | **852** Navy (background)<br>2 hanks |

☆ Middle point

150   160   170   180   190   200   210   220   230 232

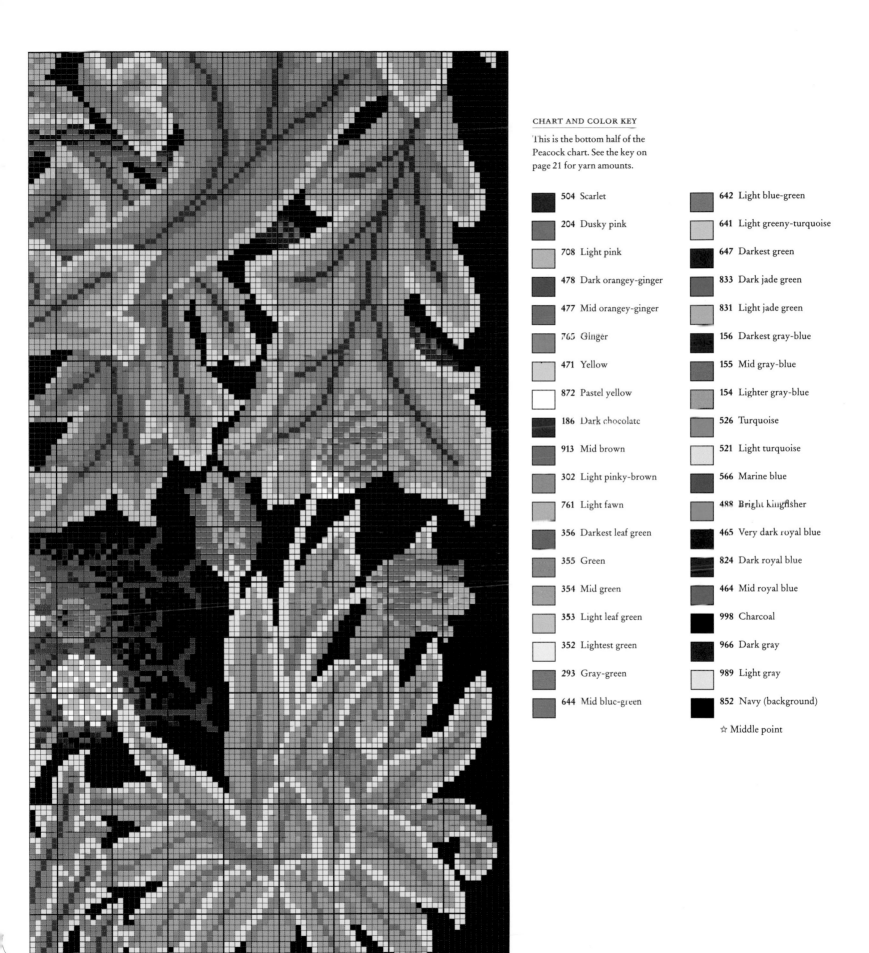

## CHART AND COLOR KEY

This is the bottom half of the Peacock chart. See the key on page 21 for yarn amounts.

| | | | | |
|---|---|---|---|
| 504 Scarlet | 642 Light blue-green |
| 204 Dusky pink | 641 Light greeny-turquoise |
| 708 Light pink | 647 Darkest green |
| 478 Dark orangey-ginger | 833 Dark jade green |
| 477 Mid orangey-ginger | 831 Light jade green |
| 765 Ginger | 156 Darkest gray-blue |
| 471 Yellow | 155 Mid gray-blue |
| 872 Pastel yellow | 154 Lighter gray-blue |
| 186 Dark chocolate | 526 Turquoise |
| 913 Mid brown | 521 Light turquoise |
| 302 Light pinky-brown | 566 Marine blue |
| 761 Light fawn | 488 Bright kingfisher |
| 356 Darkest leaf green | 465 Very dark royal blue |
| 355 Green | 824 Dark royal blue |
| 354 Mid green | 464 Mid royal blue |
| 353 Light leaf green | 998 Charcoal |
| 352 Lightest green | 966 Dark gray |
| 293 Gray-green | 989 Light gray |
| 644 Mid blue-green | 852 Navy (background) |

☆ Middle point

# Raven

EDGAR ALLAN POE describes a raven best: "In there stepped a stately Raven of the saintly days of yore ...Ghastly grim and ancient Raven wandering from the Nightly shore." What a mystical bird it is. Why, however, does it sit like an imposing punctuation at the edge of Morris's tapestry *The Forest*? In my search for an explanation I became quite fascinated, and the more I learn, the more I admire this powerful and most intelligent of birds. Ravens can live for 60 years and are said to mate for life; when one dies, a younger bird replaces it, so it could be said that the couple are immortal.

Since Noah sent it from the Ark, the raven has symbolized different things in many cultures. It can be seen on the totem poles of some Native Americans, who considered it to be the discoverer of fire. In Ireland, the raven was domesticated and its different calls were interpreted as divinations. In Christian symbolism it is Satan. In Welsh folklore, it is looked on more gently – blind people are said to recover their sight if they are kind to ravens. And a Celtic myth tells us that King Arthur may return in the form of a raven. For hundreds of years ravens have been kept in the Tower of London with their wings clipped, as legend has it that if they leave the Tower, the Kingdom will fall.

The Anglo Saxon word for raven is *Hrafn* and the chief Norse god, Odin, was also the *Hrafnagnd*, the Raven God. Now I feel we are closer to Morris, for he loved and indeed translated many of the Norse legends. Odin had two ravens and carried one on each shoulder; they were called Hugin, who represented thought, and Mugin, memory. Each day they were sent to question the living and the dead and returned before nightfall to report to their master on the state of the world.

Now I had found the inspiration and could hardly have been more enthusiastic; the interpretation was the next task. The overpowering impression left

by the raven is that it is completely black. Tackling the colors, or rather the lack of them, was a problem. Encouraged by the fact that Morris had faced the same problem with wool and had overcome it, I started to stitch. I made several birds. Using primarily black simply produced a silhouette; introducing blues and greens to indicate the sheen often resulted in a better shaped bird but the plumage was too colorful. Obviously, I could use only the darkest colors, but how was I to show the rounded wing against the head and tail, and indicate the feathers? After much time and stitching, my colleague Selina Winter hit on the idea of two "sets" of colors to differentiate between the various parts of the bird, so the wings became very slightly blue and the rest green. We had quite a lot of fun as the Raven developed. It is now just as I had wanted – strong, slightly ominous, and very mysterious.

ABOVE THIS WONDERFUL DECORATION IS FROM THE 13TH-CENTURY *ALPHONSO PSALTER*. IT HAS ALL THE EVIL HUMOR OF SOME OF WILLIAM DE MORGAN'S DESIGNS. WHAT SKILL AND IMAGINATION THESE ILLUSTRATIONS DEMONSTRATE.

FAR LEFT THE RAVEN STANDS GUARD IN FRONT OF A 16TH-CENTURY FIREPLACE IN QUEEN ANNE'S BEDROOM AT BROUGHTON CASTLE IN THE OXFORDSHIRE COUNTRYSIDE. THE CARVED HEAD RATHER REMINDS ME OF WILLIAM MORRIS!

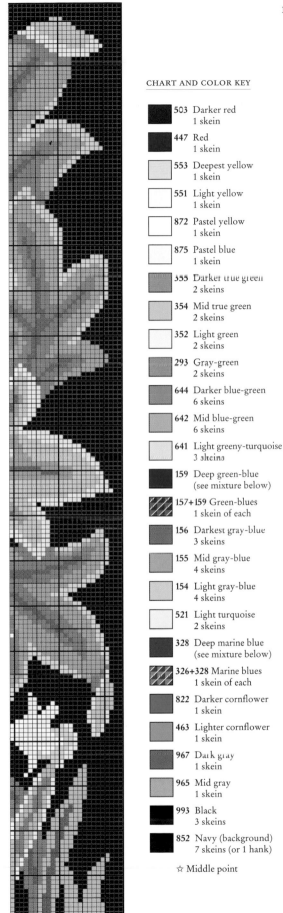

## CHART AND COLOR KEY

| | | |
|---|---|---|
| ■ | **503** | Darker red 1 skein |
| ■ | **447** | Red 1 skein |
| □ | **553** | Deepest yellow 1 skein |
| □ | **551** | Light yellow 1 skein |
| □ | **872** | Pastel yellow 1 skein |
| □ | **875** | Pastel blue 1 skein |
| ▨ | **555** | Darker true green 2 skeins |
| ▨ | **354** | Mid true green 2 skeins |
| □ | **352** | Light green 2 skeins |
| ▨ | **293** | Gray-green 2 skeins |
| ▨ | **644** | Darker blue-green 6 skeins |
| ▨ | **642** | Mid blue-green 6 skeins |
| ▨ | **641** | Light greeny-turquoise 3 skeins |
| ■ | **159** | Deep green-blue (see mixture below) |
| ▨ | **157+159** | Green-blues 1 skein of each |
| ▨ | **156** | Darkest gray-blue 3 skeins |
| ▨ | **155** | Mid gray-blue 4 skeins |
| ▨ | **154** | Light gray-blue 4 skeins |
| □ | **521** | Light turquoise 2 skeins |
| ■ | **328** | Deep marine blue (see mixture below) |
| ▨ | **326+328** | Marine blues 1 skein of each |
| ▨ | **822** | Darker cornflower 1 skein |
| ▨ | **463** | Lighter cornflower 1 skein |
| ▨ | **967** | Dark gray 1 skein |
| ▨ | **965** | Mid gray 1 skein |
| ■ | **993** | Black 3 skeins |
| ■ | **852** | Navy (background) 7 skeins (or 1 hank) |

☆ Middle point

## MATERIALS FOR THE RAVEN CUSHION

**Canvas:** 14 threads/in (5.5/cm) deluxe Zweigart mono canvas measuring 18 x 18in (46 x 46cm)

**Threads:** Appleton crewel yarn

**Needle:** Size 20 tapestry

**Finished size of design:** 14 x 14in (35.5 x 35.5cm)

**Stitch:** Tent stitch, using 3 strands of crewel yarn

This unusual design can be made into a cushion, fire screen, stool, or workbox top. On very fine canvas it would make a lovely top for a jewelery box or a really interesting book cover; it might be fun to try it in silk or cotton threads, but do make sure that you have the colors for the Raven itself before you start.

Always remember that you can change the size of the design by changing the canvas gauge. As a chair seat it would probably need to be larger, so choose a coarser canvas and be prepared to extend the foreground flowers to cover the front of the chair. Work your sizes out carefully.

The challenge of giving shape to a black bird has been met here by using two "sets" of colors and by making the lightest shade in each set by blending two colors. In the chart the greener portions of the bird are clearly defined from the bluer parts. Work the lightest shade in the greener parts with one thread of 157 and two of 159 in the needle, the next shade with three strands of 159, and the darkest shade with three strands of black (993). Similarly, in the bluer areas, work the lightest shade with one strand of 326 and two strands of 328. The chart shows clearly where the various shades in the feathers are positioned.

Work the entire pupil of the eye using black (993), and create the glint in the pupil by making a tiny cross using white sewing thread.

The large acanthus leaves in the background are worked in two "sets" of colors, the greener sides of the leaves with 156, 644, 642, and 641, the bluer sides with 156, 155, 154, and 521. All the leaf veins are worked in 156. Please note that 156 is also used in the leaves in the foreground.

THIS BEAUTIFUL RAVEN, TAKEN FROM THE WATER-COLOR PAINTED BY PHILIP WEBB FOR *THE FOREST* TAPESTRY, ACCOMPANIED THE ARTIST'S OBITUARY IN THE *ARCHITECTURAL REVIEW* OF JULY 1915. WEBB WAS A CLOSE FRIEND OF MORRIS'S AND OFTEN DREW THE BIRDS AND ANIMALS THAT WERE DEPICTED IN HIS DESIGNS.

180  190  200 204

# Lion

THE OLDEST OF heraldic symbols, the lion, looks incredibly lifelike as it moves majestically through Morris's medieval *Forest* tapestry, illustrated on pages 14-15. With his dignified self-confidence, he quite rightly takes center stage.

While Morris was at Oxford, he had been obliged to keep his hair and beard well trimmed. When he left, he quite abandoned these niceties and his hair and beard grew pretty well uncontrolled for the rest of his life. This is a description of Morris's reaction when someone made the mistake of criticizing the work of his great friend and colleague Edward Burne-Jones: "His eyes flamed as with actual fire, his shaggy mane rose like a burning crest, his whiskers and moustache bristled like pine needles, he stormed up and down the room like a caged lion." It was not the first time, nor would it be the last, that Morris was likened to the King of Beasts.

Although used to seeing films and photographs of lions, I was quite unprepared for the excitement I felt when I first saw one in the wild. At the time, I had already started work on my Lion design; he was drawn and I was at the color-choosing stage. My two-week holiday to Kenya with my husband was intended as a total break from stitching, and I had not anticipated any connection between the two. Everything about that first wild lion was so powerful – its size, the smoothness of movement, the deceptively slow turning of the head. I was awe-struck. On my return from Kenya my mind was a complete jumble of soft, sandy, smooth tones, and I was terribly anxious not to lose the precise memory of what I had seen.

The drawings for all the creatures depicted in *The Forest* had been completed some time before our trip, and the Raven, Fox, and Hare had all been stitched and sewn together as a triptych. As the Peacock's colorings were still causing me to hesitate, I decided to work on the Lion next.

The usefulness of a finished piece of stitching is not of primary importance to me; I want it to work as a piece of art in its own right. I wanted to make the Lion in the correct proportion to the other creatures. It was not until it was completed as a rather grand cushion, with the amusing fringe, that I realized what a handsome stool cover it would make, if I could only find the perfect piece of furniture. The success of the large Peacock hanging, which is shown on page 19, has given me the urge to see the Lion on that broader gauge of canvas, too. I can hardly imagine a more dramatic wall decoration.

The branches that wend through Morris's huge original weaving look a little confusing when viewed in small pieces, and I therefore omitted them in my Lion. They do make sense with the Peacock, however, because he is standing on one of them, so I included them only in that design. I also left out the motto, as there was no sensible place to put it in the divided sections. I thought a great deal about the border that frames the original tapestry so well, but I felt that it would become too dominant around the creatures on my designs and separate them more than I wanted.

The sheer size of the original did offer Morris's weavers more scope for detail. I was worried that the Lion's face might not be quite right on my needlepoint – a few stitches can result in a totally different expression or a complete lack of realism. The different textures of hair, from the light and then dark manes to the smooth, muscular back, were as difficult to achieve in their way as were the variety of colors in my Peacock design and the shades of black in my Raven.

ABOVE THIS QUAINT LION IS FROM A 15TH-CENTURY BOOK OF HOURS. THE ARTIST CANNOT HAVE BEEN WELL ACQUAINTED WITH LIONS!

FAR LEFT THIS STATELY X-CHAIR IS IRRESISTIBLE. EVERY TIME I VISIT STANDEN, IT SEEMS JUST THE PLACE TO PHOTOGRAPH A CUSHION. LION FITS IT PERFECTLY. THE WHOLE PHILIP WEBB HOUSE WAS DECORATED FOR THE BEALE FAMILY BY MORRIS & CO. IN THE 1890S.

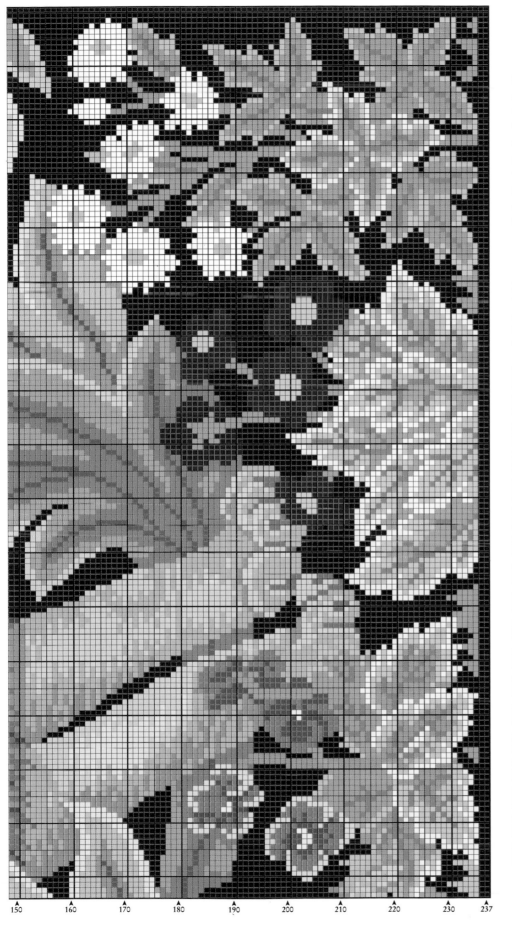

RIGHT The whiskers were
added after Lion was
completed. Buttonhole
thread, or a few strands
of sewing thread in a
natural color, can be
used to make the straight
stitches. Of course, you
can improvise — after all,
he is your lion!

## CHART AND COLOR KEY

The Lion cushion was made in
Appleton crewel yarn. The rest of
the chart and the materials needed
appear on pages 34–5.

| | |
|---|---|
| **504** Dark red — 1 skein | **352** Light green — 2 skeins |
| **501** Red — 1 skein | **293** Gray-green — 3 skeins |
| **104** Dark mauve — 1 skein | **644** Darker blue-green — 9 skeins |
| **102** Light mauve — 1 skein | **642** Mid blue-green — 8 skeins |
| **473** Deep yellow — 1 skein | **641** Light greeny-turquoise — 4 skeins |
| **472** Yellow — 1 skein | **156** Darkest gray-blue — 4 skeins |
| **695** Deep honey — 1 skein | **155** Mid gray-blue — 6 skeins |
| **692** Light honey — 1 skein | **154** Light gray-blue — 7 skeins |
| **872** Pastel yellow — 1 skein | **521** Light turquoise — 4 skeins |
| **581** Dark chocolate — 1 skein | **463** Mid cornflower — 1 skein |
| **186** Chocolate — 1 skein | **462** Light cornflower — 1 skein |
| **913** Dark fawn — 3 skeins | **561** Light blue — 1 skein |
| **903** Ginger — 3 skeins | **998** Charcoal — 1 skein |
| **902** Gold-brown — 6 skeins | **974** Elephant gray — 1 skein |
| **901** Light gold-brown — 5 skeins | **984** Light beige — 1 skein |
| **761** Mid beige — 2 skeins | **991B** White — 1 skein |
| **355** Dark true green — 2 skeins | **852** Navy (background) — 16 skeins (or 2 hanks) |
| **354** Mid true green — 4 skeins | |

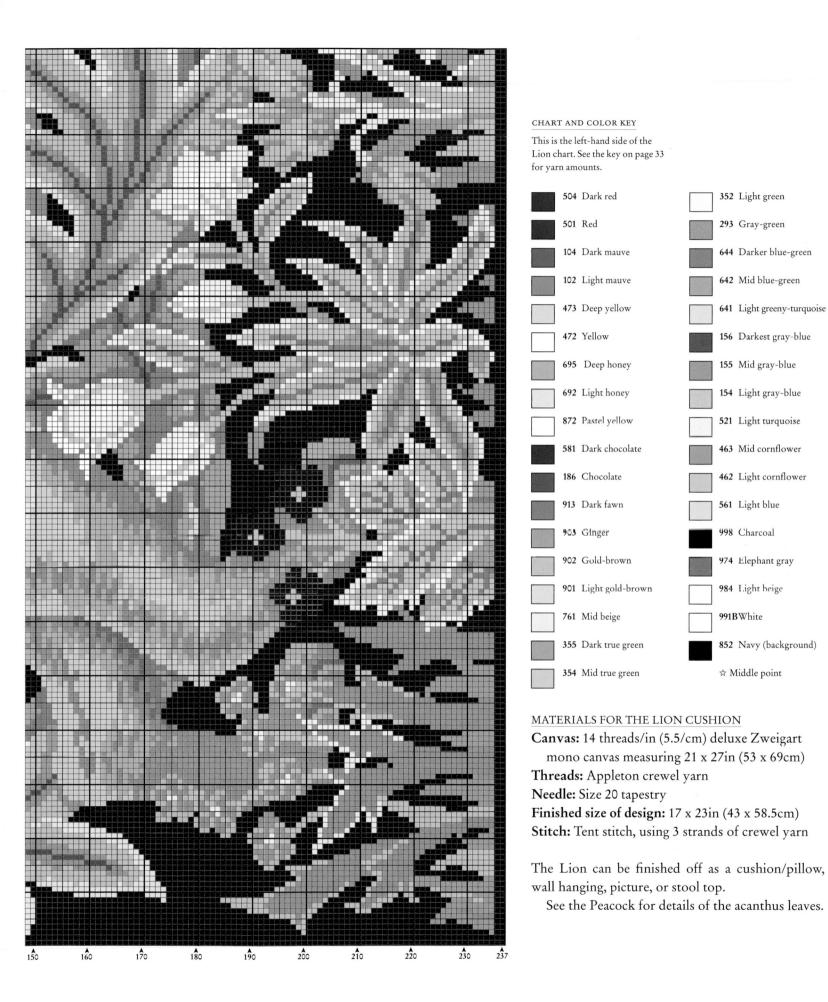

CHART AND COLOR KEY

This is the left-hand side of the Lion chart. See the key on page 33 for yarn amounts.

| | | | | |
|---|---|---|---|---|
| 504 | Dark red | | 352 | Light green |
| 501 | Red | | 293 | Gray-green |
| 104 | Dark mauve | | 644 | Darker blue-green |
| 102 | Light mauve | | 642 | Mid blue-green |
| 473 | Deep yellow | | 641 | Light greeny-turquoise |
| 472 | Yellow | | 156 | Darkest gray-blue |
| 695 | Deep honey | | 155 | Mid gray-blue |
| 692 | Light honey | | 154 | Light gray-blue |
| 872 | Pastel yellow | | 521 | Light turquoise |
| 581 | Dark chocolate | | 463 | Mid cornflower |
| 186 | Chocolate | | 462 | Light cornflower |
| 913 | Dark fawn | | 561 | Light blue |
| 903 | Ginger | | 998 | Charcoal |
| 902 | Gold-brown | | 974 | Elephant gray |
| 901 | Light gold-brown | | 984 | Light beige |
| 761 | Mid beige | | 991B | White |
| 355 | Dark true green | | 852 | Navy (background) |
| 354 | Mid true green | | ☆ | Middle point |

MATERIALS FOR THE LION CUSHION

**Canvas:** 14 threads/in (5.5/cm) deluxe Zweigart mono canvas measuring 21 x 27in (53 x 69cm)

**Threads:** Appleton crewel yarn

**Needle:** Size 20 tapestry

**Finished size of design:** 17 x 23in (43 x 58.5cm)

**Stitch:** Tent stitch, using 3 strands of crewel yarn

The Lion can be finished off as a cushion/pillow, wall hanging, picture, or stool top.

See the Peacock for details of the acanthus leaves.

150    160    170    180    190    200    210    220    230    237

# FLOWERY
# MEADES

_H_nd as we slipped between the lovely summer

greenery I almost felt my youth come back to me...

when I was too happy to think that there could be

much amiss anywhere

_News from Nowhere_, 1890

A DETAIL FROM A DREAMY VIEW OF _OXFORD FROM HINKSEY HILL_, PAINTED BY WILLIAM TURNER (1789-1862). MORRIS WAS VERY HAPPY IN THIS MEDIEVAL CITY DURING HIS UNDERGRADUATE DAYS. IN 1877, HE WAS INVITED TO BECOME PROFESSOR OF POETRY, BUT HE DECLINED.

MORRIS ENTERED OXFORD UNIVERSITY in 1853 at the age of nineteen. It was here that he met all the people who were to have the greatest influence on his future. With a group of very close friends, this was a time of uninhibited enjoyment – political discussions, poetry readings, practical jokes, enormous comradeship, and the burgeoning of all the gifts that Morris was to develop so fully.

At the Oxford entrance examination Morris sat next to Edward Burne-Jones and their friendship and artistic collaboration were to last a lifetime. Their studies, ostensibly to enter the Church, provided less of an inspiration than did the atmosphere of Oxford – "an astounding, romantic and medieval city," rich in architecture, art, literature, and history. The summer vacation that they spent together walking in France, rhapsodizing about cathedrals and churches, established their joint enthusiasm for "a life of Art," and at the time Morris wrote a gentle letter to his mother explaining, "I do not hope to be great at all in anything but perhaps I may reasonably hope to be happy in my work and sometimes when I am idle and doing nothing, pleasant visions go past me of the things that may be." Morris was rarely to be found doing nothing, but he retained the ability to see pleasant visions all his life. His mother had to wait many years before he was to find his true destiny.

Morris believed that architecture was the basis of all art and so, after completing his ecclesiastical studies (to please his mother), he apprenticed himself to G. E. Street, the architect responsible for the gothic-style Law Courts in the Strand, London. Here, Morris formed a close and lasting friendship with Philip Webb, who was destined to design both his married home, Red House at Bexleyheath, and his tombstone at Kelmscott.

Like a shadow, the Pre-Raphaelite painter Dante Gabriel Rossetti entered Morris's life and his influence can hardly be underestimated. He tutored Burne-Jones in the art of painting and it was not long before he had seduced Morris to join them in lodgings in Red Lion Square, London, where they were all to paint. Morris's mother was distraught at yet another change of direction in her son's career and unjustly blamed Burne-Jones.

The summer of 1857 was spent at Rossetti's suggestion back at Oxford. He introduced his new young model, 16-year-old Jane Burden, to the group, and Morris fell immediately and lastingly in love. Her strange beauty was much admired and it was this that provided her with a passport from her poor family background to the fashionable world of the Pre-Raphaelites. Although "Janey" was to say

later in life that she never loved Morris, they were married in Oxford, two days after his 25th birthday.

Around the time of his marriage, deeply in love and very happy, Morris eagerly made plans with Philip Webb for his dream house; this was Webb's first commission. They found the perfect site in an orchard, which was only a short train journey away from London. Although he was to remain there for only five years, it is at Red House that we see the most complete picture of Morris. This cozy home, where the gardens and orchard flowed into the house, was where his children were born, where Burne-Jones and his wife Georgiana, Rossetti and his wife the painter Lizzie Siddal, and many other friends spent weekends painting walls, ceilings, and furniture. There was much discussion, reading aloud, eating, drinking, and playing of games.

While at Red House, Morris at last found his way; he abandoned painting and, as he said, became a "decorator," With a £100 loan from his mother, Morris and his friends – Burne-Jones, Rossetti, Webb, Ford Madox Brown, Marshall, and Faulkner – formed "The Firm." This multitalented group wished to re-create the standards of craftsmanship lost in the Industrial Revolution. At their premises in Red Lion Square, all the partners and their families were involved in making stained glass, furniture, embroidery, carving, and metalwork, and their creative business was often continued at weekends at Red House.

Morris planned to move the whole enterprise to Red House and hoped that Burne-Jones and family would move in, too. Webb prepared plans for an extension to the house. Tragically, ill health struck the Burne-Jones', and not having the cushion of financial security that Morris had, they decided not to leave London. Morris was bitterly disappointed and later confessed that he had cried at the news.

In the autumn of 1865 the Morris family sadly took leave of their perfect home and moved with the business, which had outgrown Red Lion Square, to Queen Square, London. Red House featured much in their dreams, but they were never to return.

# African Marigold

THE BEAUTY OF the painted design for Morris's *African Marigold* fabric is its exquisite delicacy of line and color; I found it breathtaking when I first saw it at the William Morris Gallery. The large blue leaves look as if they are being blown by a breeze – this marvelous movement, interwoven with the smaller foliage, can only be a Morris creation.

Morris had a passion for color and he was extremely knowledgeable about it. We can only imagine his anger when he discovered that the colors he so admired in old fabrics belonged to a lost age, that the relatively new chemical dyeing had eradicated all trace of old methods. The new colors were not just unpleasant but unstable.

Characteristically, when Morris first decided to develop his own dyes, he turned to old books to learn how to dye with madder, walnut shells, indigo, and other natural ingredients. He set up experiments in the scullery at his home in Queen Square and, in fact, dyed embroidery threads there.

The manager of "The Firm" was George Wardle, whose brother Thomas owned a dyeing factory in Leek, Staffordshire. Their father had been a renowned silk dyer who had used the old methods 30 years earlier but, sadly, had taken much of the knowledge to his grave. Thomas Wardle was as keen as Morris to rediscover his father's skill.

Morris, exhibiting the usual uninhibited eagerness that emerged each time he worked on a new project, spent weeks at a time in Leek, more often than not in the dye house. He happily refers to himself as a dyer's mate and describes a morning helping Thomas Wardle and four others dye 20 pounds of silk in a copper vat six feet wide, sunk nine feet into the ground. For three years, Morris's hands were almost permanently blue, which caused great hilarity among his friends and a certain amount of embarrassment to him when he returned to the London social scene.

Blue was Morris's favorite color and it was intended that the *African Marigold* fabric be dyed blue using the "indigo discharge" method – a process requiring a great deal of skill. At first, this method proved to be most elusive. Thomas Wardle was always very anxious to please the exacting Morris, but he failed in the final printing of *African Marigold*. After five months of experimentation with indigo, he must have despaired and used the much cruder Prussian blue. Morris, of course, let his disappointment be known. The harsh colors of that printing were as different as they could be from the gentle blues in the original painting. Morris had to wait until he moved his company to Merton Abbey before he successfully printed with indigo.

Interestingly, the first time that *African Marigold* appeared in front of the public was as a silk version under Thomas Wardle's name at the Paris Exhibition in 1878. Nowadays the fabric is still produced by Liberty of London in a variety of colors, including a soft gray-blue.

*African Marigold* has, of course, a repeating pattern, but a glance at the painting always puts me in mind of a rug. Several years ago I produced a cushion using the central flower and loved the result, pleased that I had retained the delicate feel of the watercolor. This made the development of my rug design much easier. I tipped the central flower upright for the sake of symmetry. The small repetitive climbing leaves in the border do not compete with the generous swirls of the center and frame the rug gently.

ABOVE MY INSPIRATION FOR THE AFRICAN MARIGOLD RUG. I LOVE THIS BEAUTIFUL WATERCOLOR AND PENCIL DRAWING, WHICH MORRIS DID IN 1876. YOU CAN SEE IT AT THE EXCELLENT WILLIAM MORRIS GALLERY IN WALTHAMSTOW, LONDON.

FAR LEFT THE RUG SOFTENS THE MAGNIFICENT STONE FLOOR OF THE ORANGERY AT HESTERCOMBE HOUSE, SOMERSET.

CHART AND COLOR KEY

The African Marigold rug was
made in Appleton tapestry yarn.
The rest of the chart appears on
pages 46-7.

| | | |
|---|---|---|
| | **693** Deeper yellow<br>3 skeins | **641** Light greeny-turquoise<br>2 hanks |
| | **692** Soft yellow<br>1 skein | **521** Light turquoise<br>4 hanks |
| | **691** Dirty ivory<br>6 hanks | **325** Darkest marine blue<br>5 hanks + 3 skeins |
| | **901** Light brown<br>3 skeins | **324** Dark marine blue<br>5 hanks |
| | **354** Clear green<br>3 hanks | **322** Mid marine blue<br>1 hank |
| | **296** Dark gray-green<br>1 hank | **321** Light marine blue<br>11 hanks |
| | **294** Mid gray-green<br>4 hanks + 3 skeins | **876** Very pale blue<br>1 hank |
| | **293** Light gray-green<br>5 hanks + 3 skeins | **992** Ivory (background)<br>8 hanks |

☆ Middle point

MATERIALS FOR THE AFRICAN MARIGOLD RUG

**Canvas:** 8 threads/in (3/cm) Zweigart interlock
rug canvas measuring approximately 48 x 67in
(122 x 170cm)

**Threads:** Appleton tapestry yarn

**Needle:** Size 16 tapestry

**Finished size of design:** 42 x 61in (106.5 x 155cm)

**Stitch:** Cross stitch, using one strand of tapestry yarn

This chart by Ethan Danielson is a masterpiece. I am
always amazed at how he manages to indicate the
different colors so clearly without losing their
subtlety. The design is not symmetrical, so it is
charted here in its entirety. I am thrilled to see the
large rug miniaturized – and what a pretty dressing-
room stool it would make.

Please note that 692 appears as the stamens of the
central flower only. 521 is the main shade in the
lighter petals of the four blue flowers, and also
appears in the wreaths and next to the very pale blue
in the central flower. 641 is the main shade in the
darker petals of the four blue flowers and is around
the veins in the central flower.

## CHART AND COLOR KEY

This is the rest of the African Marigold chart. See the key on page 45 for yarn amounts.

| | | | |
|---|---|---|---|
| **693** Deeper yellow | | **641** Light greeny-turquoise | |
| **692** Soft yellow | | **521** Light turquoise | |
| **691** Dirty ivory | | **325** Darkest marine blue | |
| **901** Light brown | | **324** Dark marine blue | |
| **354** Clear green | | **322** Mid marine blue | |
| **296** Dark gray-green | | **321** Light marine blue | |
| **294** Mid gray-green | | **876** Very pale blue | |
| **293** Light gray-green | | **992** Ivory (background) | |

☆ Middle point

200  210  220  230  240  250  260  270  280  290  300  310

# Flower Border

IN THE MAJORITY of Morris & Co.'s commissions – whether they were tapestries, stained glass, or illustrations – Morris himself designed the borders. He had this wonderful ability to pull things together, to frame the work appropriately. His borders are beautiful but, unlike his backgrounds, which frequently take on an importance as great as the subject, they do not overshadow or dominate – just complement the centers. As with all great designs, they can also stand on their own. It was only after I had focused on the honeysuckle border around his own *Woodpecker* tapestry that I properly appreciated this skill and set myself to study Morris's borders for their own sakes.

Once involved in this hungry hunt for borders, I could not stop, and produced the designs for my Honeysuckle, Orange, and Flower Borders in quick succession. I was more interested in the result of the stitching than what to do with the needlepoints when complete. After three designs and five cushions – the result of my experimenting with background colors – I reluctantly listened to the pleas of my family and friends about a limit to the need for bolster-size cushions. However, these three Border cushions, as I now call them, have kept me enthralled, and I know I could keep busy designing variations for a considerable time.

My drawing of the Flower Border had been lying idle in my studio for longer than I care to remember. As with many things that I consider very special, I tend to save them for a suitable occasion. Unlike the Honeysuckle and Orange Borders, this is clearly intended as a border only – not as a frame for something else. The flowers are too powerful to play second fiddle to another design.

Morris had an intense interest in plants; even under pretty adverse conditions during a stay in Iceland he was able to note down and name the wild plants growing there. Everything in his design work was based on nature. His first design for embroidery was an absolutely simple and realistic sprig of daisies. Later in life, his drawings became more complex, his plants were enlarged or diminished or twisted and changed to suit the design. The flowers in this border design are rather tropical-looking and can be seen in much of Morris's and also Henry Dearle's work.

My first interpretation of the Flower Border was a large bolster cushion, and I do like the soft background. However, it had always seemed to me to be intended as a carpet or rug. I wanted to see it as large as possible and the worry now was to find a canvas wide enough. I was rather reluctant to use the 1¼ strands/in canvas that was so perfect for the large Peacock hanging, shown on page 19; two strands of Appleton tapestry yarn were adequate for a hanging but perhaps not for a rug, which might receive rather more wear. At 6 threads/in, the widest canvas I could find was 40in (1m), and when I had added a border, making the total width 255 stitches, the rug would measure a little more than this. However, 6 threads/in is perfect for two strands of tapestry yarn, so once again I called Zweigart, who in my view make the best canvas. They helped me out by sending a length of their very wide 6 threads/in canvas and we were able to make the striking rug shown overleaf. An alternative might have been to join the border to the sides of the canvas after stitching – or use a slightly finer canvas and make a slightly smaller rug.

ABOVE THE *TREE PORTIÈRE* TAPESTRY BY HENRY DEARLE. THE UNUSUAL FLOWERS CAN ALSO BE SEEN IN MEDIEVAL TAPESTRIES AND MORRIS'S WORK. THIS IS A FINE EXAMPLE OF IRREGULAR FRAMING WITH A DEEPER BASE.

FAR LEFT THE FLOWER BORDER CUSHION AT WEST DEAN, SUSSEX.

49

200  210  220  230  240  250  260  270  280  290 294

CHART AND COLOR KEY
The Flower Border cushion was made in Appleton crewel yarn, the rug in tapestry yarn. Quantities for the cushion are given first, followed by quantities for the rug.

| | | | |
|---|---|---|---|
| ■ | **127** Dark terracotta 2 skeins/38 skeins | ■ | **294** Darkest green 4 skeins/12 skeins |
| ■ | **125** Mid terracotta 2 skeins/7 skeins | ■ | **355** Mid green 6 skeins/19 skeins |
| ■ | **123** Light terracotta 4 skeins/12 skeins | □ | **352** Light gray-green 7 skeins/24 skeins |
| □ | **121** Pale terracotta 4 skeins/13 skeins | ■ | **326** Dark marine blue 1 skein/3 skeins |
| ■ | **223** Deep pink 2 skeins/7 skeins | ■ | **324** Mid marine blue 3 skeins/9 skeins |
| ■ | **222** Mid pink 3 skeins/14 skeins | ■ | **322** Light marine blue 2 skeins/6 skeins |
| ■ | **221** Light pink 2 skeins/7 skeins | ■ | **742** Pale blue 2 skeins/6 skeins |
| ■ | **241** Light olive green 1 skein/2 skeins | ■ | **052** Navy (background) 4 hanks/32 hanks or 875 Pastel gray-blue |
| □ | **331** Light yellowy-green 2 skeins/6 skeins | ☆ | Middle point |
| □ | **872** Pastel yellow 1 skein/3 skeins | | |

## MATERIALS FOR THE FLOWER BORDER CUSHION

**Canvas:** 14 threads/in (5.5/cm) deluxe Zweigart mono canvas measuring 20 x 25in (51 x 64cm)

**Threads:** Appleton crewel yarn

**Needle:** Size 20 tapestry

**Finished size of design:** 16 x 21in (40.5 x 53cm)

**Stitch:** Tent stitch, using 3 strands of crewel yarn

## MATERIALS FOR THE FLOWER BORDER RUG

**Canvas:** 6 threads/in (2.4/cm) Zweigart interlock rug canvas measuring 46½ x 58in (118 x 147cm)

**Threads:** Appleton tapestry yarn

**Needle:** Size 16 tapestry

**Finished size of design:** 35 x 47in (89 x 119cm)

**Finished size of rug:** 40½ x 52in (103 x 132cm)

**Stitch:** Cross stitch, using 2 strands of tapestry yarn

There is the equivalent of six skeins in each hank of tapestry yarn, if you prefer to buy it in hanks.

To make the outside edge of the rug, which is not shown on the chart, stitch five rows of the background color outside the design, followed by five rows of dark terracotta (127), then ten rows of the background color again.

# Honeysuckle Border

THE WOODPECKER TAPESTRY is unique. It is the only tapestry designed entirely by Morris and there is only one example of it. Measuring an impressive 9½ft (2.9m) in height, it was woven at Merton Abbey in 1885 and was displayed at the first Arts & Crafts Exhibition in 1888. Now we are fortunate enough to be able to view it in the William Morris Gallery at Walthamstow.

The *Woodpecker* tapestry is unique, too, in that there is nothing else remotely like it. Morris did not believe in copying; he liked to take the elements that pleased him, such as a plant or a color or a style, and produce something individual and totally original. We can see the influence of medieval designs in the acanthus leaves and the orange tree, but Morris has used them so differently and added his own poem and, of course, the border.

Honeysuckle was a favorite of Morris's. He first used it in a design he made for Janey to embroider and we can see it meandering through many of his designs. He made it rather a secondary feature in the printed linen called *Honeysuckle*, produced at Merton Abbey in 1876 by Thomas Wardle. May, his daughter, used it in the best of her three wallpapers.

Honeysuckle is an ideal plant for decoration. As well as being extremely pretty, its delicate soft shades will blend with most colors. It also climbs and curls naturally so that it can be made to appear anywhere in a design.

On both sides of Morris's *Woodpecker* tapestry there is honeysuckle climbing a branch. I had already been tempted by this pretty scene and stitched it many years ago as a bell pull. Now I wanted to see how it would look as a complete frame. Phyllis Steed, who does the initial sketches for many of my designs, provided a superb drawing that quite solved the problem of how best to maintain the flow of the design around each corner. Interestingly, it takes a while to notice

Morris's honeysuckle around the *Woodpecker*, but how dominant it is framing a small space on my Honeysuckle Border cushion. Like the Flower Border design, this would make a lovely rug.

Each time I stitched a different background, I looked at the Border designs afresh (and I must confess I looked eagerly at some new ones, too). They are totally versatile, a fact that I'd quite missed when making up the cushions. The designs can be used upright as fire screens or lengthwise on a stool, as well as cushions. They can be reduced in size to frame a picture or a mirror, or greatly enlarged to make a rug. They can be dominant or delicate. With a little ingenuity you can change the proportions of the frame by elongating two sides.

The very light background on one version of the Honeysuckle Border initially disappointed me as I felt that I had lost the flowers; but now having lived with it, I like it more – nothing is really lost and I find its subtlety very restful. The background in the dark version is a color that always surprises me; it never looks the same when stitched as it does in the hand. It can look mauve or brown, depending on the design colors it surrounds. When I worked the sample of Honeysuckle with the Bees inset, I tried yet another background color, the soft blue Appleton 324, which allows the bees to show up well without backstitching an outline.

ABOVE THE *WOODPECKER* TAPESTRY ALONE IS WORTH A JOURNEY TO THE WILLIAM MORRIS GALLERY.

FAR LEFT TWO OF THE HONEYSUCKLE BORDER CUSHIONS, SHOWING WHAT A DIFFERENCE BACKGROUND COLORS CAN MAKE.

CHART AND COLOR KEY

The Honeysuckle Border cushion
was made in Appleton crewel yarn.

| | | |
|---|---|---|
| | 706 | Pink 4 skeins |
| | 702 | Light pink 3 skeins |
| | 877 | Pastel pink 3 skeins |
| | 854 | Mid coral 2 skeins |
| | 861 | Light coral 2 skeins |
| | 913 | Brown 2 skeins |
| | 902 | Mid fawn 3 skeins |
| | 901 | Light fawn 2 skeins |
| | 294 | Mid gray-green 3 skeins |
| | 292 | Light gray-green 6 skeins |
| | 355 | Mid real green 3 skeins |
| | 354 | Light clear green 5 skeins |
| | 352 | Pale green 8 skeins |
| | 935 | Dark mauve (background) 4 hanks + 1 skein or 875 Pastel gray-blue |

☆ Middle point

ABOVE A DETAIL FROM
MORRIS'S *WOODPECKER*
TAPESTRY, WITH ITS
HONEYSUCKLE BORDER.

MATERIALS FOR THE HONEYSUCKLE
BORDER CUSHION

**Canvas:** 14 threads/in (5.5/cm) deluxe Zweigart
    mono canvas measuring 20 x 25in (51 x 64cm)
**Threads:** Appleton crewel yarn
**Needle:** Size 20 tapestry
**Finished size of design:** 16 x 21in (40.5 x 53cm)
**Stitch:** Tent stitch, using 3 strands of crewel yarn

This chart shows 935 (dark mauve) as the
background color, although 875 (pastel gray-blue)
or 324 (soft blue) can be used instead. The pastel
gray-blue background can be seen on the cushion
illustrated on page 54.

# Orange Border

THE BEAUTIFUL ANGELI LAUDANTES is one of a pair of magnificent Morris tapestries, each showing two angels on a millefleurs background surrounded by lovely fruit borders. Burne-Jones designed the angels originally for stained glass windows in the South Choir at Salisbury Cathedral in 1878.

Morris, Marshall, Faulkner & Co. ("The Firm") had now become Morris & Co. and had moved to much larger premises at the rather romantic Merton Abbey in south London. Once in these spacious surroundings, Morris was able to devote a long, sunny, ground-floor room to weaving. With three looms and up to nine people, he was ready for what proved to be a boom in the demand for wall hangings for both homes and churches.

The first two tapestry designs produced by Morris & Co. were called *Flora* and *Pomona*, each depicting a romantic female figure dressed in flowing robes. They proved very popular, sold well and were subsequently produced in a variety of different sizes and with different backgrounds. Burne-Jones was the principal designer for Morris & Co. and it was he who drew these figures. *Angeli Laudantes* and *Angeli Ministrantes* share some similarities with *Flora* and *Pomona*, so it is not surprising that Morris wanted to see if they would work well as tapestries, too. Sixteen years after their conception in 1878, they were woven.

As the illustrations provided by Burne-Jones were usually of figures no more than 15in (38cm) high, they were photographically enlarged to the required size. In the early years, Morris would add his wonderfully flamboyant backgrounds and borders. Later, this became the responsibility of Henry Dearle, Morris's first tapestry apprentice, who, in turn, became the teacher of the many great weavers to emerge from Merton Abbey. Although Dearle was tremendously influenced by Morris – and sometimes their work is mistaken –

Dearle did, in fact, develop a style of his own. The delicate millefleurs in the backgrounds of both the *Angeli* tapestries are unmistakably his.

However, it was the border of *Angeli Laudantes* that first attracted me. The ever-present, all-enveloping acanthus leaves wend their way around, allowing a glimpse of an orange or blossom or fresh green leaves to relieve their drama. There are very few people who are able to "layer" a design so successfully and these borders have all the hallmarks of Morris. It is thought by some that at the time the tapestries were woven, Morris was so involved with his Kelmscott Press that he had stopped designing for tapestry. In the end it is of little importance. The Orange Border makes a most dramatic cushion, and tempted though I have been, it is not yet a rug! I know it would look wonderful.

The border of *Angeli Ministrantes* is every bit as tempting as its partner's. The acanthus is still there, with pomegranates and slightly pinky blossoms instead of oranges – delicious! Both hangings have a luminescence that never seems to show in photographs; they are well worth searching out and enjoying.

The *Angeli* tapestries were first exhibited in 1890 by the Arts & Crafts Exhibition Society in Manchester. The Victoria & Albert Museum in London bought *Angeli Laudantes*, while *Angeli Ministrantes* rather disappeared into private ownership. Happily, they have now been reunited and can be seen at the V & A.

ABOVE THE *ANGELI LAUDANTES* TAPESTRY. THE ANGELS WERE ORIGINALLY DESIGNED BY BURNE-JONES FOR STAINED GLASS WINDOWS, BUT BY 1894 WALL HANGINGS HAD BECOME FASHIONABLE AND THE DESIGN WAS USED AGAIN – WITH AN ADDED BORDER – FOR TAPESTRY.

FAR LEFT ORANGE BORDER CUSHION IN THE GARDENS OF HESTERCOMBE HOUSE.

## CHART AND COLOR KEY

The Orange Border cushion was made in Appleton crewel yarn.

- **477** Rust — 2 skeins
- **474** Golden yellow — 2 skeins
- **473** Mid yellow — 2 skeins
- **471** Light yellow — 2 skeins
- **991B** White — 4 skeins
- **355** Darkest green — 2 skeins
- **353** Mid green — 4 skeins
- **351** Light gray-green — 3 skeins
- **874** Light mint green — 2 skeins
- **644** Darker blue-green — 5 skeins
- **642** Mid blue-green — 6 skeins
- **641** Light greeny-turquoise — 3 skeins
- **156** Darkest gray-blue — 3 skeins
- **155** Mid gray-blue — 6 skeins
- **154** Light gray-blue — 7 skeins
- **521** Light turquoise — 4 skeins
- **852** Navy (background) — 4 hanks
- ☆ Middle point

ABOVE A BORDER DETAIL FROM *ANGELI LAUDANTES*.

## MATERIALS FOR THE ORANGE BORDER CUSHION

**Canvas:** 14 threads/in (5.5/cm) deluxe Zweigart mono canvas measuring 20 x 25in (51 x 64cm)

**Threads:** Appleton crewel yarn

**Needle:** Size 20 tapestry

**Finished size of design:** 16 x 21in (40.5 x 53cm)

**Stitch:** Tent stitch, using 3 strands of crewel yarn

So far, I have experimented with three different blue backgrounds – pastel gray-blue (875), indigo (926), and navy (852).

# Bees

ONE OF THE CRITICISMS of my Border designs had been that there was a hole in the middle of each one. I pointed out that this was because they were borders and that if I filled in the centers, they might lose their purpose. However, the criticism must have niggled me and, determined to justify my choice, I pondered on the puzzle of the Border centers and how I could possibly fill them.

Our younger son Paul was in favor of bees. I was rather hesitant as they did not spring to mind as being very "Morrisy," but I tried them out and am now rather fond of them. They give the Orange Border cushion, shown on the left, a summery feel. Here you see four bees, worked in tent stitch, but you should decide how many to have and their positions for yourself. It is easier to make these decisions after completing the design and, of course, before the background is stitched.

The wings of bees are actually transparent and I have tried to give this effect by stitching two strands of white (991B) blended with one of light greeny-turquoise (641). With the exception of black, all the colors are to be found in the yarns for the Orange Border and you will almost certainly have sufficient. However, with the Honeysuckle Border cushion, you will need a skein of each of the four colors.

I have not tried stitching anything in the center of the Flower Border. The flowers are very distinctive and seem quite complete in themselves – however, one can never be certain!

I have had great fun with the backgrounds of these cushions. An old favorite of mine, Appleton 926, is close to Morris's indigo and looks wonderful with the oranges, but even though it is lighter than the original navy (852), it did not allow the bees to show clearly. So, I worked a line of backstitching around the black parts of the bees with a light sewing thread. Should you find the bees disappearing on a very light background, try backstitching around the lighter areas with a dark sewing thread. They show well against soft blue (324), which I used for one of the Honeysuckle Border cushions, but I would not suggest this color for the other Border cushions as it is too close to some of the actual design colors.

ABOVE A SURREAL DETAIL FROM A 12TH-CENTURY ENGLISH BESTIARY. THESE BEES RETURNING TO THE APIARY MAKE ME SMILE EACH TIME I SEE THEM – THEY ARE RATHER MORE ORDERLY THAN MINE!

FAR LEFT THE PARTIALLY STITCHED ORANGE BORDER CUSHION, WITH THE BEES ALREADY COMPLETED, PHOTOGRAPHED IN THE FURNITURE DEPARTMENT OF LIBERTY IN LONDON.

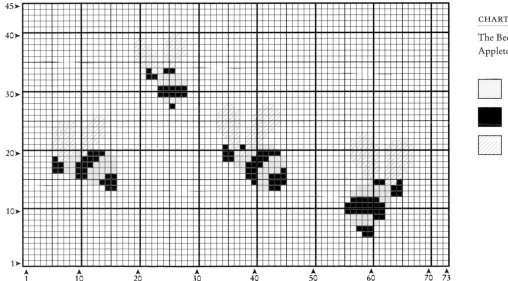

**CHART AND COLOR KEY**

The Bees inset was made in Appleton crewel yarn.

- 471 Yellow
  1 skein
- 993 Black
  1 skein
- 991B +641 White + Light greeny-turquoise
  1 skein of each

# Arts & Crafts Alphabet

THE BORDER CUSHIONS look very handsome with plain backgrounds, but should you wish to add some detail you could choose your own center – add your initials or stitch the Bees shown on page 65, for example. This Arts-&-Crafts-style alphabet could also be stitched in tent stitch in a different color before working the background. However, I liked the subtle embossed look achieved by stitching over the already completed background using the same color. The single flower motif is taken from a decorative space-filler frequently used by Morris in his Kelmscott Press publications.

Whether you are going to work the tent stitch or the embossed letters, it is vital that you plan the positioning carefully, preferably using squared paper. Find the center of the cushion and baste along the horizontal and vertical centre lines with colored sewing thread. Use sewing thread, too, to indicate exactly where you want to position each letter.

The stitching is easy. For the embossed look, use three strands of crewel yarn; make long, horizontal stitches over the background tent stitch, following your chart. Note that where the required stitch was too long to be practical, I have used two shorter stitches instead. One square on the chart is the equivalent of one background tent stitch. Try to keep the tension of your long stitches even. One extra skein of the background yarn shade should be sufficient to stitch four letters.

For clarity, the letters on the chart are in yellow. If you want the embossed effect, these stitches should naturally be the same color as your background.

FAR LEFT THE ORANGE BORDER CUSHION WITH A VERY PALE BACKGROUND AND MORRIS'S INITIALS AND FLOWER AT HESTERCOMBE HOUSE, SOMERSET.

☆ Middle points

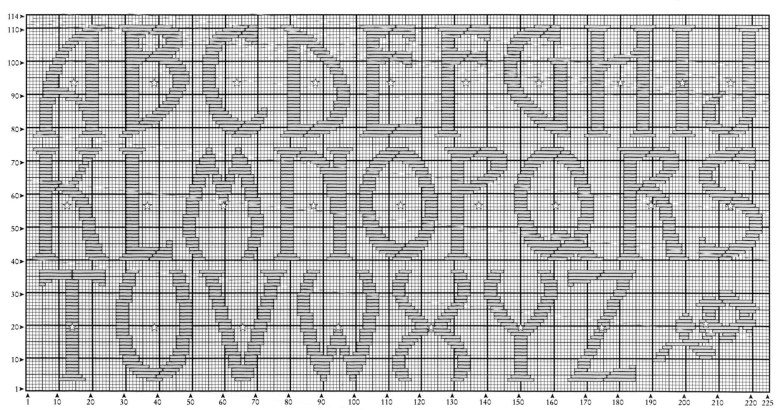

# FRUITS OF LABOR

# Che thing which I understand by real art is the expression by man of his pleasure in labour. I do not believe he can be happy in his labour without expressing that happiness

*The Art of the People*, 1879

IT IS REMARKABLE HOW MANY ASPECTS OF MORRIS'S LIFE SEEM TO BE DEPICTED IN THE PAINTING *PENELOPE* BY JOHN RODDAM SPENCER – THE VERY PRE-RAPHAELITE WOMEN WITH THEIR LOOSE HAIR AND FLIMSY SOFT CLOTHING, THE GARDEN AND ORCHARD, AND OF COURSE, A PARTIALLY WORKED TAPESTRY OF A MEDIEVAL SCENE.

IN THE AUTUMN OF 1865, Morris returned to the part of London he knew so well. The family moved into a large house in Queen Square, Bloomsbury, which they shared with "The Firm." In effect, Morris was living above the shop and able to devote all his working hours to experimenting with natural dyeing techniques, practicing calligraphy, designing his first three wallpapers, translating Icelandic sagas, writing poetry and, of course, running the now flourishing business.

During this time, through Rossetti's influence, a very prestigious commission was obtained to decorate part of St James's Palace. Lizzie Siddal, Rossetti's wife, had by now killed herself after losing a child and Rossetti was spending more and more time with Janey. Morris commissioned a portrait of her, but I suspect that by the time it was completed Rossetti and Janey's indiscreet relationship had become too distressing for Morris to appreciate the painting, with its unkind inscription. This portrait is shown on page 41.

Morris, in his usual positive and blunt way of dealing with life, went in search of a country house to share with Rossetti. It seems an extraordinarily kind and sensible act to present Janey and Rossetti with the opportunity to be together without causing a scandal. Intended only as a weekend holiday home, Kelmscott Manor in Oxfordshire was to replace Red House in Morris's life and dreams.

It was a sixteenth-century house, which he described as an idyllic home. He loved the garden and spent hours on the river and walking in the countryside.

Morris and Rossetti shared the lease and it was Rossetti who moved in with Janey and the children in July 1871 while Morris went to Iceland. Rossetti was never as fond of Kelmscott Manor as Morris. He, like another of Janey's lovers fourteen years later, found the corridors creaky and the landscape flat, although this did not deter either of them from spending time there with Janey. It is sad that the house, which should have been Morris's perfect medieval haven, was somewhere from which he was on occasions forced to escape. We can argue that had his private life been more content, Morris might have had less reason to channel his enormous energy into so many creative avenues. And we can only reflect on how much poorer we would have been.

By 1872, it was apparent that "The Firm" needed even more space. Morris moved his family's London home from Queen Square to Horrington House in Turnham Green near Chiswick. Webb referred to it as "the little shed on the High Road." Janey found it too small, but Morris was content there for the next six years. He was closer to "The Grange" where Burne-Jones lived, and a routine developed that was to last twenty years – each Sunday Morris would join the Burne-Jones's for a huge breakfast and then spend the following few hours with his old friend discussing books, art, and life.

The words on the banner read: "O valiant earth O happy year that works the threat of winter year and hangs aloft from tree to tree the banners of the spring to be"

THE ORCHARD TAPESTRY,
SHOWING FOUR MAIDENS IN
AN ORCHARD OF ORANGES,
APPLES, GRAPES, AND PEARS,
WAS ADAPTED FROM A DESIGN
BY MORRIS FOR A PAINTED
CEILING IN JESUS COLLEGE
CHAPEL, CAMBRIDGE. THE
WORDS ON THE BANNER ARE
FROM ONE OF HIS POEMS.
HENRY DEARLE DESIGNED
THE BACKGROUND.

Back at Queen Square the family scullery became Morris's dye works and a carpet loom was erected upstairs so that he could learn the hand-knotting techniques used in Persian rugs. Rossetti was almost permanently at Kelmscott Manor during 1872-3, which proved too much for Morris. He wrote a disappointed letter to Rossetti enclosing his share of the rent and suggesting that Rossetti take over the whole payment in future.

For the first time in his life, Morris's financial situation was insecure. The value of the shares that his father had left him had steadily declined. Now it was essential that "The Firm" continue to thrive and Morris felt that he needed to have total control of the company. His six partners were no longer

directly involved in its running, but Rossetti and Brown, now both occupied with their painting, and Marshall the engineer wanted to remain partners. There followed some bitter wrangling, and Morris eventually agreed to pay each partner £1,000 for their shares. His good friends Burne-Jones, Webb, and Faulkner all waived their claims, but Rossetti cruelly asked that his share be paid to Janey.

So, May 1875 saw the end of Morris, Marshall, Faulkner & Co. ("The Firm") and the start of Morris & Co. with Morris as the owner. He wrote to his mother: "I have got my partnership business settled at last and am sole Lord and Master now." It was Morris who renewed the lease at Kelmscott Manor and Rossetti was seen less frequently there.

# Apples

PART OF THE ENORMOUS attraction of Morris's designs is their abundant detail. The eye passes hungrily from foreground to background and back again, perceiving more detail each time.

We know about some of Morris's methods of working from his lectures. All his designs were very carefully considered before reaching paper and each drawing, he tells us, should have "beauty, imagination and order." Henry Dearle was his best known pupil and so absorbed his master's ideals that many of his designs have been taken as Morris's. Dearle drew the backgrounds for the *Orchard* and *Pomona* tapestries, which are illustrated in this book, and it was these that first inspired my Apples design. I love the richness of the fruit and the dense foliage in these tapestries. They make me think of Morris's happy days in Epping Forest and his beloved Red House, built in an orchard.

Creating the dense foliage in my Apples was to prove something of a challenge. To show the shape of each leaf as it lies on another can be difficult in tent stitch. At first, I thought that I could achieve this effect only by using an enormous number of different greens and, in fact, I colored and re-colored this design many times before deciding it was quite feasible. I work with colored pencils, attempting to match the Appleton wools I am thinking of using. This helps me to decide on the number of colors I need to keep the shapes distinct in each part of the design. In spite of the wide variety of pencils now available, I can never find the range of colors that I do in the wool yarns, so the intended shades of some of the drawn colors remain in my mind's eye until stitched.

Next came the decision about the apples – which variety? There are surely many more found in modern times than were growing in Victorian gardens. I stitched a very deep red apple, shading to yellow on the less ripe side.

The first examples of my new needlepoint designs are usually stitched by my colleague Selina Winter, who is infinitely more skillful with the needle than I and who taught me so much when I was at the Royal School of Needlework. When I visited her during the early stages of my Apples design, it was with armfuls of stitched pieces, drawings, masses of yarns, and pounds of apples to put with her bowl of Cox's Orange Pippins. We discussed the green leaves and examined the apples. This is always an enjoyable time for me; I have done my soul-searching and can now delegate with enthusiasm.

Earlier, when discussing the Border cushions, I mentioned how much a background can change the appearance of a design. It is normally the last decision to be made and it is always nerve-racking. So much effort goes into the completion of a design that it would be heart-breaking to choose a background that does not do it justice. Colors change when used over a large area and, in turn, alter the colors of the stitching they surround; my tendency is to return to the security of my tried and tested backgrounds. Blue sky seemed a sensible background for a tree, but what shade? I finally settled on a mixture of two blues, and now I'm taken with the idea of creating clouds and adding more shades of blue, as I once did with a design taken from a window by Tiffany.

ABOVE *POMONA*, WHICH WAS WOVEN AT MERTON ABBEY, IS A BURNE-JONES FIGURE WITH A TYPICAL DEARLE BACKGROUND.

FAR LEFT I WAS DELIGHTED TO HAVE THE *ST AGNES* TAPESTRY AS A BACKGROUND FOR MY APPLES DESIGN AT STANDEN IN SUSSEX.

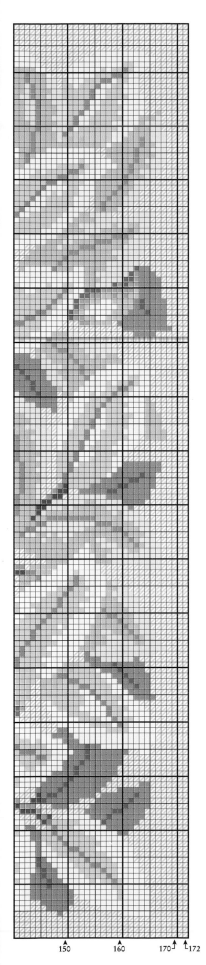

## CHART AND COLOR KEY

The Apples design was made in Appleton tapestry wool with the background in crewel yarn.

| | | |
|---|---|---|
| ■ | **725** | Dark red<br>1 skein |
| ■ | **722** | Soft red<br>1 skein |
| ■ | **205** | Pink<br>1 skein |
| ■ | **473** | Dark yellow<br>1 skein |
| □ | **996** | Lemon<br>1 skein |
| ■ | **914** | Brown<br>1 skein |
| ■ | **912** | Light brown<br>1 skein |
| ■ | **547** | Darkest green<br>1 skein |
| ■ | **545** | Bright clear green<br>1 skein |
| ■ | **543** | Light clear green<br>1 skein |
| □ | **542** | Light gray-green<br>3 skeins |
| ■ | **255** | Dark yellowy-green<br>5 skeins |
| ■ | **252** | Yellowy-green<br>6 skeins |
| □ | **251A** | Light yellowy-green<br>6 skeins |
| ▨ | **561+876** | Pale + Pastel blues<br>(background)<br>8 skeins of 561<br>4 skeins of 876 |

☆ Middle point

**ABOVE** MORRIS'S *APPLES* DESIGN FOR WALLPAPER.

## MATERIALS FOR THE APPLES DESIGN

**Canvas:** 12 threads/in (5/cm) deluxe Zweigart mono canvas measuring 18 x 18in (46 x 46cm)

**Threads:** Appleton tapestry and crewel yarns

**Needle:** Size 18 tapestry

**Finished size of design:** 14 x 14in (35.5 x 35.5cm)

**Stitch:** Tent stitch, using one strand of tapestry yarn or 3 strands of crewel yarn

It is hard to believe but, at the time of writing, I have still not made Apples into anything. Perhaps I am subconsciously waiting for the perfect piece of furniture to display it, a Victorian pole screen (a fire screen on a pole to shield the face from heat) or a table with a drop-in glass top. On page 74, Apples can be seen on a table frame, which is said to have belonged to May Morris. In the background of this picture taken at Standen, you can see the *St Agnes* tapestry hanging on the stairway. Webb built the house for the Beale family and each detail of his and the Morris & Co. furnishings is a treat to see.

The main part of the Apples design was stitched in tent stitch, using one strand of tapestry yarn in the needle. The background was worked in crewel yarn, blending two strands of pale blue (561) and one strand of pastel blue (876) in the needle.

# Vine

MORRIS'S VINE DESIGN brings to mind bacchanalian feasts, good health, hospitality, and happiness. There are several references in Morris's life to occasions when he was seen with bottles of wine in his arms in jovial mood determined to celebrate, either with friends at Red House or to drink to the health of the new Kelmscott Press. It is rather alarming that the careful, concerned financial manager of "The Firm," Warrington Taylor, once wrote to Morris warning him to make economies in his household expenditure and to contain his own wine consumption to £80 a year, or two and a half bottles a day! We can take heart remembering the amount of entertaining that Morris undertook.

The vine is a decoration that has been used through the ages; its curving stems are perfectly malleable and can be wrapped around pedestals or draped across doorways. The flat leaves and the rotund grapes lend themselves wonderfully to carving, we see them in marble, stonework, and wood in old buildings all over the world. They are symbols of plenty. Morris used the vine extensively in his woodcuttings for the Kelmscott Press.

*Vine* was produced as a wallpaper in 1874. It is a brilliant design, one of Morris's best. The vine seems quite random, so cleverly is the repeat hidden. Morris lectured that the true test of a good design is if the pattern covers the ground equally and richly. In *Vine* he used willow as a backdrop. We are not surprised to learn that he said, "the more and the more mysteriously you interweave your sprays and stems the better."

At first I found it difficult to establish the scale for my version of Morris's *Vine*. I could not decide how much of the piece to show and how large to make the grapes. Then there were other decisions to make – which color version to follow, the olive or blue leaf variety – and finally the all-powerful, all-changing background color. As usual, Phyllis Steed

battled her way brilliantly around the problems created by taking only a part of a design. Morris lectured severely on the importance of "rational growth" and "that no stem should be so far from its parent stock as to look weak." It is important for everything to make sense and that stems appear from somewhere logical.

I decided on the blue vine leaves in the end because the blue binds the leaves more to the grapes and allows the soft green willow to act as a better ground to them both. As to the grapes, it took a great deal of stitching on my "scrap" canvas before I was happy. I produced several bunches – some small, some large and luscious, some black, green, and purple. The colors are subtle and the bloom deceptively difficult. One of the bunches that I had bought to study had a mixture of black and red grapes, and this gave me the idea of using the two colors.

The dark olive background was an experiment which worked well. Arthur Sanderson & Sons offer two weights of furnishing fabrics using Morris's original *Vine* wallpaper design; they have used this olive background and I thought I would like to try it. It has made my design really dramatic.

As soon as I saw the Arts & Crafts fire screen, I wanted to show it in this book – it looks so like the work of the architect C. F. A. Voysey, one of Morris's contemporaries, who also designed fabrics, wallpapers, and furniture.

ABOVE MORRIS'S ORIGINAL PENCIL AND WATERCOLOR DESIGN OF *VINE* IS NOW AT THE VICTORIA & ALBERT MUSEUM IN LONDON.

FAR LEFT HOW APT TO SEE MY VINE IN FRONT OF THE FAMOUS WEBB FIREPLACE AT RED HOUSE. MORRIS, JANEY AND FRIENDS SPENT MANY LONG AND HAPPY WEEKENDS IN THIS ROOM, PLAYING HIDE-AND-SEEK, READING ALOUD, AND EMBROIDERING.

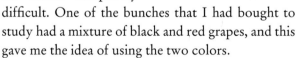

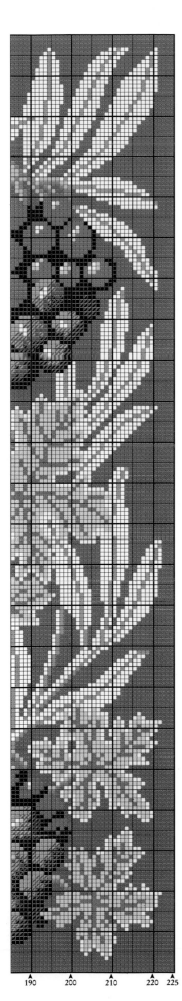

### CHART AND COLOR KEY

The Vine fire screen was made in Appleton crewel yarn.

| | | |
|---|---|---|
| | 913 | Dark fawn<br>1 skein |
| | 901 | Light fawn<br>1 skein |
| | 355 | Mid green<br>4 skeins |
| | 352 | Light green<br>8 skeins |
| | 156 | Dark blue-green<br>5 skeins |
| | 154 | Mid green-blue<br>8 skeins |
| | 521 | Light turquoise<br>4 skeins |
| | 852 | Darkest blue<br>2 skeins |
| | 326 | Dark blue<br>2 skeins |
| | 321 | Mid gray-blue<br>1 skein |
| | 921 | Light gray-blue<br>1 skein |
| | 935 | Dark mauve<br>2 skeins |
| | 714+935 | Mauves<br>(see single colors) |
| | 714 | Mid mauve<br>2 skeins |
| | 714+932 | Mauves<br>(see single colors) |
| | 932 | Light dull mauve<br>2 skeins |
| | 244 | Dark olive<br>(background)<br>4 hanks |

☆ Middle point

## MATERIALS FOR THE VINE FIRE SCREEN

**Canvas:** 14 threads/in (5.5/cm) deluxe Zweigart mono canvas measuring 25 x 20in (64 x 51cm)

**Threads:** Appleton crewel yarn

**Needle:** Size 20 tapestry

**Finished size of design:** 16 x 15¾in (40.5 x 40cm)

**Stitch:** Tent stitch, using 2 strands of crewel yarn

Vine was stitched using just two strands of crewel yarn in the needle, which is sufficient for some stitchers. However, I have given yarn estimates as if three strands are used. With three strands the color blending will be a little different and will give you room to experiment for yourself. The background was worked using three strands.

The black grapes are stitched with 921 as an occasional highlight, 321 as the lightest color or the bloom, 326 as the main color, and 852 as the shadow. The red grapes are made with a variety of color mixes, not all appearing in each grape. They have 321 again as the highlight, 932 as the lightest color; then the stitches can be of 932 and 714 blended, all 714, or 714 and 935 blended. All the shadows are solid 935.

When Vine was first stitched, it was too small for the fire screen, but happily it was on a large piece of canvas, and I considered enlarging it by using the chart and repeating some of the fruit and leaves. Edward and Doris Hollamby had kindly agreed to allow us to take photographs in Red House, but there just was not enough time to finish it before our visit. Florentine stitch was the perfect solution. It has a marvellous texture and is quick to do, worked over four threads of canvas using four strands in the needle. Vine would also look superb made up as a cushion with a thick, flamboyant cord or as a chair seat. It was an exciting coincidence to find that the Hollambys had covered their chair in a fabric of the same design.

ABOVE MORRIS'S *VINE* DESIGN FOR TEXTILES.

190 200 210 220 225

# Artichoke

ANOTHER TREASURE to cherish at the William Morris Gallery in Walthamstow is the first example of Morris's embroidered panel called *Artichoke*. The embroidery, which was executed by Ada Phoebe Godman, looks clean and uncluttered in spite of the complexity of the design; the colors are particularly appealing. I really covet this. It would be fascinating to see how a wall of these lovely panels would serve to soften the harsh angles of modern homes. There are few, I fear, who would have the patience to find out. I can only marvel at that of Mrs Godman, whose diary records her eagerness to get started in August 1877 and who, in 1900, was still stitching one of the many *Artichoke* panels she made! It was the practice then, as it is today, for groups of friends and family to stitch together, and I can only hope that she had some help.

Morris was introduced to the art of embroidery by G. E. Street, the architect. As with everything, Morris strove to learn the techniques before he started designing. He collected old embroidered fabrics and unpicked the threads to learn the stitches. He practiced on an embroidery frame copied from an old one until he was confident he had mastered the art. Popular at the time was Berlin work – cross stitch worked on canvas from a chart – but both Street and he felt that it was too rigid a discipline which did not allow enough room for creativity.

Anxious as always to share his knowledge, Morris then taught the housekeeper at his home in Red Lion Square. "Red Lion Mary," as she was known, was made to bring her embroidery frame to work so that Morris could note and, no doubt, comment on her progress. Later Janey, her sister Bessie, Georgiana Burne-Jones, and Charles Faulkner's wife and sister (and others!) were shown the delights of long and short stitch and of laying and couching, which stitches to use and how to place them – in fact, all the complexities of free

embroidery. Morris's preferred medium was wool, both for backing and thread. As early as 1857 he was having his threads dyed specially for him.

In their early days at Red House, Morris and Janey embroidered clumps of daisies onto indigo-dyed serge to hang around the bedroom walls. They created a fashion among their friends in which embroidered panels became part of the interior decor.

Embroidery of all kinds was offered in "The Firm's" first catalog. The work was done by the friends and relations of the partners, supervised by Janey and her sister. Morris was delighted by Janey's natural ability with the needle. He also encouraged Elizabeth Wardle, the wife of his dye specialist, to learn to embroider. He sent her some old pieces to unpick as he had done and offered to design her a carpet. She responded and was responsible for setting up the Leek School of Embroidery. The Royal School of (Art) Needlework had Morris as one of its very first designers.

Each of Morris's enterprises is like a stem. We can watch it grow, strengthen, branch out and produce fruit. His influence on the development of embroidery as a recognized art form was enormous, and through this he helped to change the general perception of women. Stitching was considered no more than a respectable way for ladies to occupy themselves. By elevating embroidery to an art form

ABOVE ONE OF SEVERAL *ARTICHOKE* PANELS THAT WERE EMBROIDERED BY MRS ADA GODMAN.

FAR LEFT *ARTICHOKE* AS A CHAIR SEAT BY THE ORIEL WINDOW IN THE DRAWING ROOM AT RED HOUSE, WHERE JANEY AND FRIENDS WOULD SIT AND EMBROIDER.

which both men and women could enjoy, he helped to alter the way that the world viewed women and, more importantly, he altered the way that women perceived themselves.

In the 1890s, when Morris and Janey were living in Kelmscott House, the home of their married daughter May was a few doors away and was the center of the Morris & Co. embroidery business. May supervised a much larger group of assistants than had her mother in Red Lion Square. Among them were the sisters of W. B. Yeats and William De Morgan, and Annie Jack, the wife of Morris's chief furniture designer. As in all Morris's workplaces, the pay was better than average and the atmosphere seems to have been relaxed, with the river only a few yards away. Morris made casual daily visits. Here, commissions for completed embroideries were undertaken and embroidery kits produced.

*Artichoke* proved to be one of the most popular of Morris's designs for embroidery. It could be supplied ready to be traced onto linen as it was for Mrs Godman, or as a kit with part of the design already worked to indicate the placing of the colors and the type of stitch. It was Philip Webb who obtained the *Artichoke* design commission from Mrs Godman for Morris. He was by then a well-known architect and often recommended Morris's furnishings for the interiors of his houses. He had completed Smeaton Manor in 1876, and it was there that Mrs Godman hung her *Artichoke* panels.

Another famous Webb house is Standen in East Grinstead, built for the Beale family. It is now preserved with much of its Morris interiors intact and is looked after by the National Trust. Margaret Beale and her daughter also stitched a version of *Artichoke*. They completed two matching panels in silk in different colorings from the wool hangings. It is interesting to see how well both versions work. I wonder how much the silk has faded over the years and exactly what it looked like in 1877.

There are four distinct repeating motifs in Morris's *Artichoke* panel, linked by the ogival terracotta root and interspersed as always with pretty meandering plants. Dismissing my dreams of wall hangings meant that I could use only parts of the original for my design, unless I stitched something incredibly fine. The dominant blue flower is an awkward shape, too tall for a square design and not tall enough for a fire screen. The artichoke surrounded by the pink cup flowers is most attractive and seemed a natural starting point. The root that connects the whole design makes little sense on its own and detracts from the overall design, so I left it out in favor of the tiny background flowers. Completed on the easily stitched 12 threads/in canvas, my Artichoke makes a full and elegant chair seat. I wondered about the practicality of the light background, but it was the whole color scheme that had originally pleased me and I could not bear to risk spoiling it.

I now realized that my second Artichoke design was going to look rather strikingly different from the first. As I had dismissed thoughts of the impractical large blue flower, my choice lay between the smaller blue flower and the pale group of artichoke bulbs. I finally opted for the latter but know that I will not be able to resist the other for long. The colors in Mrs Godman's hangings vary slightly, presumably to avoid the tedium of repeating herself, but it had been her panel in the William Morris Gallery that had first attracted me and the extremely pale greens on the off-white background were a challenge.

The problem with outlining in needlepoint is the different thicknesses one achieves according to the angle of the stitch. In crewel work this does not occur, as one can lay the stitch in its natural direction. I tried the pale artichokes without the outline and with many shadings. I was worried that Artichoke II would look insignificant next to Artichoke I and that with far less blue and pink in the former, they would not look like a pair. They are different, of course, but blend well together as I should have expected, and they have retained some of the clarity I had so liked in the original at Walthamstow. I wonder how the third one will affect the set.

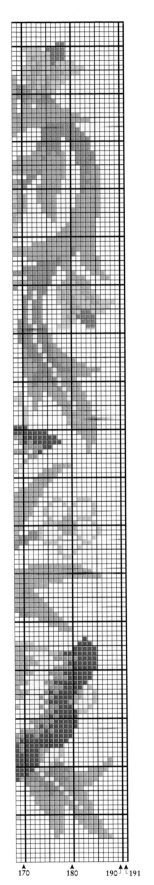

**CHART AND COLOR KEY**

The Artichoke I cushion was made in Appleton tapestry yarn.

- **223** Dark pink
  1 skein
- **222** Mid pink
  1 skein
- **221** Light pink
  2 skeins
- **122** Dull browny-pink
  2 skeins
- **331** Pale yellowy-green
  1 skein
- **402** Darkest green
  4 skeins
- **401** Mid green
  5 skeins
- **874** Mint green
  1 skein
- **873** Pastel green
  1 skein
- **926** Dark bright blue
  2 skeins
- **525** Dark dull blue
  1 skein
- **323** Mid blue
  3 skeins
- **321** Light marine blue
  4 skeins
- **152** Light gray-blue
  3 skeins
- **876** Pastel blue
  5 skeins
- **992** Off-white
  (background)
  2 hanks

☆ Middle point

ABOVE A DETAIL FROM MORRIS'S *ARTICHOKE*, WHICH INSPIRED MY FIRST ARTICHOKE DESIGN.

MATERIALS FOR THE ARTICHOKE I CUSHION

**Canvas:** 12 threads/in (5/cm) deluxe Zweigart mono canvas measuring 19 x 20in (48 x 51cm)

**Threads:** Appleton tapestry yarn

**Needle:** Size 18 tapestry

**Finished size of design:** 14½ x 16in (37 x 40.5cm)

**Stitch:** Tent stitch, using one strand of tapestry yarn

The dark blue in the center of this Artichoke design gives it dramatic depth, and it has such a clean-cut look that it would enhance most things. On 12 threads/in (5 threads/cm) canvas it is a very good size for most chair seats, with plenty of design and not too much background. I should also like to see it on top of a workbox or as a footstool.

Please note that the center of the artichoke bulb should be worked in pastel green (873).

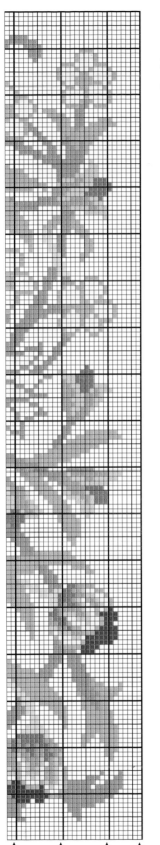

**CHART AND COLOR KEY**

The Artichoke II cushion was
made in Appleton tapestry yarn.

| | | |
|---|---|---|
| ■ | **223** | Dark pink<br>1 skein |
| ■ | **221** | Light pink<br>1 skein |
| ■ | **122** | Dull browny-pink<br>3 skeins |
| □ | **331** | Pale yellowy-green<br>1 skein |
| ■ | **402** | Darkest green<br>5 skeins |
| ■ | **401** | Mid green<br>6 skeins |
| □ | **352** | Light green<br>1 skein |
| □ | **874** | Mint green<br>4 skeins |
| □ | **873** | Pastel green<br>1 skein |
| ■ | **323** | Mid blue<br>2 skeins |
| ■ | **321** | Light marine blue<br>2 skeins |
| □ | **152** | Light gray-blue<br>3 skeins |
| □ | **876** | Pastel blue<br>3 skeins |
| □ | **992** | Off-white<br>(background)<br>2 hanks + 1 skein |

☆ Middle point

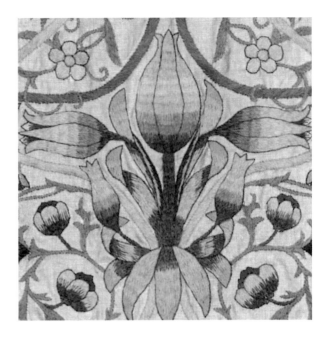

ABOVE A DETAIL FROM<br>
MORRIS'S ARTICHOKE, WHICH<br>
INSPIRED MY SECOND<br>
ARTICHOKE DESIGN.

**MATERIALS FOR THE ARTICHOKE II CUSHION**

**Canvas:** 12 threads/in (5/cm) deluxe Zweigart
mono canvas measuring 19 x 20in (48 x 51cm)

**Threads:** Appleton tapestry yarn

**Needle:** Size 18 tapestry

**Finished size of design:** 15 x 16in (38 x 40.5cm)

**Stitch:** Tent stitch, using one strand of tapestry yarn

This pretty design makes an interesting partner for
Artichoke I, as either a cushion or a chair seat. Its soft
coloring tempts me to try a darker background; I
would want to experiment before committing myself,
but it is an exciting prospect. Its delicacy would also
lend itself to fine linen and silk threads. Once I
concentrate on the shape of a design, dozens of
applications come to mind – all one needs is the time!

Please note that the centers of the artichokes
should be worked in pastel green (873).

# Fruit

FRUIT, OR POMEGRANATE, is one of the group of three wallpapers Morris designed in Red Lion Square, just a year after the founding of "The Firm" in 1861. They were in defiance of the rather regimented heraldic papers available from Pugin and Owen Jones, which Morris enthusiastically disliked. The other two designs were called *Trellis* and *Daisy*. *Trellis* was based on the rose trellis at Red House, with birds said to be designed by Philip Webb; *Daisy* was reminiscent of the hangings Morris and Janey had stitched for their bedroom there.

These three designs are quite different from the wallpapers we most usually associate with Morris. The complex, curving, multilayered designs were not produced until the 1870s, Morris's most prolific "wallpaper" period. They covered the walls of many fashionable houses in Britain. From old photographs we can peep into the past and see *Daisy* decorating a bedroom in the Burne-Jones family home and *Trellis* in Morris's bedroom at Kelmscott House. We know that *Fruit* and Rossetti's painting of Janey were in the dining room of Kelmscott House. The familiarity of these papers makes me feel closer to that time – now a century away.

Peaches, oranges, lemons and pomegranates – all featuring in Morris's *Fruit* wallpaper – would have been seen in the conservatories of the larger Victorian houses and, I am sure, considered very stylish. I have tried unsuccessfully to grow a small orange tree at home and have recently found some tiny lemons from which I am hoping to cultivate a little plant from the pips – another dream!

The pomegranate fascinated the Victorians, including Morris. It appears frequently in all forms of art of this time. The ripe fruit was a symbol of fertility and perhaps a lady holding one could be defined as a temptress. Rossetti drew a series of paintings of Janey holding a pomegranate, the most famous of which can be seen on the left.

Morris's *Fruit* wallpaper was produced in a variety of colorways, with light, gray, and sky blue backgrounds, as illustrated below, covered with a fine tracery of irregular stems. The pomegranates and peaches have matching leaves, as do the oranges and lemons. Unlike the other fruits, which are shown in profile, the pomegranates appear from all angles and in different degrees of ripeness. *Fruit* is a very romantic paper with a medieval air and exotic fruit to remind us of sunny lands. The effect it has on a room is that of a shady corner of a lush garden.

The *Fruit* wallpaper had been on my mind for eight years. It is a favorite of Phyllis Steed and graces the wall of her and her husband Robert's pretty sitting room. It is she who is responsible for the lovely line drawings that are so often the start of a new project of mine. She finally grew tired of waiting for me to produce a kit based on this Morris wallpaper and stitched her own cushion. I was terrifically intrigued to see that, virtually free-handing it onto the canvas, she had made it so like the wallpaper that when placed against it the eye quite lost the cushion. All the naiveté and rather flat colors were captured perfectly.

When I wanted a series of small but simple designs, *Fruit* sprang to mind again. Now I could see what I would do with the colors. As usual, I outlined parts of the design on to my "scrap" canvas and stitched away, trying different greens for the leaves and yellows for the lemon, and so on. Whenever I am working out colors, I stitch and then leave the stitching in a prominent place so that I can glance at it, or study it, or see it accidentally.

ABOVE ONE OF THE VERSIONS OF *FRUIT*, OR *POMEGRANATE*, DESIGNED BY MORRIS & CO. AND PRODUCED BY JEFFREY & CO. IN 1861.

FAR LEFT *PROSERPINE*, PAINTED BY ROSSETTI IN 1874, ONE OF EIGHT VERSIONS OF JANEY AS THE RELUCTANT QUEEN OF HADES. THIS PORTRAIT DATES FROM JUST AFTER THE TIME ROSSETTI VIRTUALLY MOVED INTO KELMSCOTT MANOR WITH JANEY AND THE CHILDREN.

I find it helps me to make up my mind about it. I can remember my father placing half-completed paintings in the center of my mother's carefully polished and tidied sideboard where they might remain for days, even weeks, to her dismay.

I was disappointed when I saw that I had made my plants far too realistic. This should have been a case of "less is more," but I had used too many colors and overelaborated. I had no intention of copying Phyllis Steed's version; I was quite determined to make it myself. I stole another look at her cushion and started again.

In the meantime our elder son Nick had devised a program that enabled me to design on the computer. I had first tried it when designing the Kelmscott Frame, as shown on page 104, and although I was working with the unfamiliar cotton threads, it had turned out well. This seemed the perfect solution. Now I could experiment with colors without stitching unsuccessfully for weeks. I battled for a

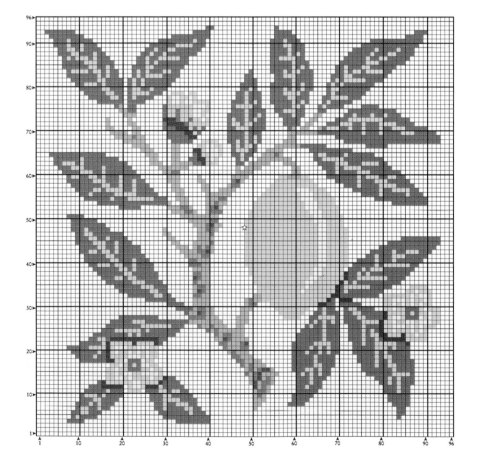

## CHART AND COLOR KEY

The Lemon cushion was made in Appleton tapestry yarn.

| | | | | |
|---|---|---|---|---|
| | **842** Yellow 1 skein | | | **241** Olive green 1 skein |
| | **331A** Soft greeny-yellow 1 skein | | | **296** Dark green 1 skein |
| | **913** Brown 1 skein | | | **294** Mid green 3 skeins |
| | **911** Mid fawn 1 skein | | | **352** Light gray-green 1 skein |
| | **951** Light fawn 2 skeins | | | **992** Off-white (background) 9 skeins |

☆ Middle point

## MATERIALS FOR THE LEMON CUSHION

**Canvas:** 12 threads/in (5/cm) deluxe Zweigart mono canvas measuring 12 x 12in (30 x 30cm)
**Threads:** Appleton tapestry yarn
**Needle:** Size 18 tapestry
**Finished size of design:** 8 x 8in (20 x 20cm)
**Stitch:** Tent stitch, using one strand of tapestry yarn

while – my computing skills leave a lot to be desired – often changing my mind about leaf-vein colors and the shapes of the branches, but feeling confident.

Finally, off to the stitchers went the four little canvases, fewer shades of yarn than before and the rather smart new charts.

The simplicity of my Fruit designs gives them great versatility and, while waiting for their return from the stitchers, I decided to try the Lemon on linen. The surprising result is that the cross stitch has the primitiveness I sought originally, whereas the wool cushions are all still looking rather realistic. However, I do think they are pretty and should like to see them all in cotton threads, like the Lemon shown on the workbox on page 119. On much coarser canvas, all four Fruit designs might also make a rather charming tiled rug.

RIGHT ORANGE ON A DECORATIVE ROSSETTI CHAIR.
FAR LEFT LEMON ON THE BED IN THE WILLOW BEDROOM
AT STANDEN IN SUSSEX.

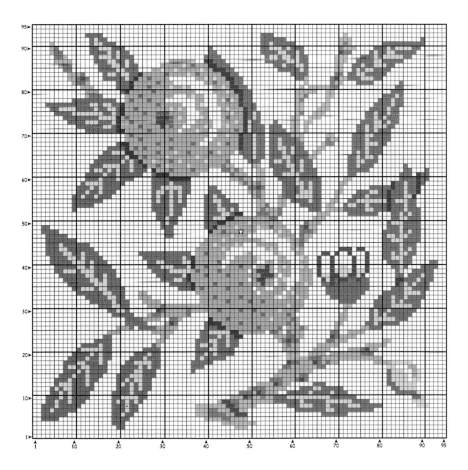

## CHART AND COLOR KEY

The Orange cushion was made in Appleton tapestry yarn.

| | | |
|---|---|---|
| 476 | Dark orange | 1 skein |
| 474 | Mid orange | 2 skeins |
| 872 | Pastel yellow | 1 skein |
| 913 | Brown | 1 skein |
| 911 | Mid fawn | 1 skein |
| 951 | Light fawn | 2 skeins |
| 241 | Olive green | 1 skein |
| 296 | Dark green | 1 skein |
| 294 | Mid green | 3 skeins |
| 352 | Light gray-green | 1 skein |
| 992 | Off-white (background) | 9 skeins |

☆ Middle point

## MATERIALS FOR THE ORANGE CUSHION

**Canvas:** 12 threads/in (5/cm) deluxe Zweigart mono canvas measuring 12 x 12in (30 x 30cm)

**Threads:** Appleton tapestry yarn

**Needle:** Size 18 tapestry

**Finished size of design:** 8 x 8in (20 x 20cm)

**Stitch:** Tent stitch, using one strand of tapestry yarn

MATERIALS FOR THE PEACH AND
POMEGRANATE CUSHIONS
**Canvas:** 12 threads/in (5/cm) deluxe Zweigart
  mono canvas measuring 12 x 12in (30 x 30cm)
**Threads:** Appleton tapestry yarn
**Needle:** Size 18 tapestry
**Finished size of design:** 8 x 8in (20 x 20cm)
**Stitch:** Tent stitch, using one strand of tapestry yarn

CHART AND COLOR KEY

The Peach cushion was
made in Appleton tapestry yarn.

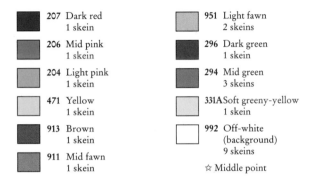

| | | |
|---|---|---|
| **207** Dark red 1 skein | | **951** Light fawn 2 skeins |
| **206** Mid pink 1 skein | | **296** Dark green 1 skein |
| **204** Light pink 1 skein | | **294** Mid green 3 skeins |
| **471** Yellow 1 skein | | **331A** Soft greeny-yellow 1 skein |
| **913** Brown 1 skein | | **992** Off-white (background) 9 skeins |
| **911** Mid fawn 1 skein | | ☆ Middle point |

CHART AND COLOR KEY

The Pomegranate cushion was
made in Appleton tapestry yarn.

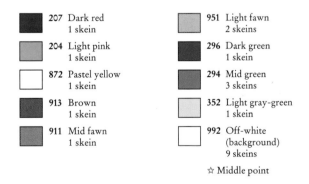

| | | |
|---|---|---|
| **207** Dark red 1 skein | | **951** Light fawn 2 skeins |
| **204** Light pink 1 skein | | **296** Dark green 1 skein |
| **872** Pastel yellow 1 skein | | **294** Mid green 3 skeins |
| **913** Brown 1 skein | | **352** Light gray-green 1 skein |
| **911** Mid fawn 1 skein | | **992** Off-white (background) 9 skeins |
| | | ☆ Middle point |

FAR RIGHT STANDEN IS FULL OF SURPRISES. HERE WE HAVE THE
ORIGINAL MORRIS *FRUIT* WALLPAPER TO SHOW OFF THE PEACH
AND POMEGRANATE CUSHION.

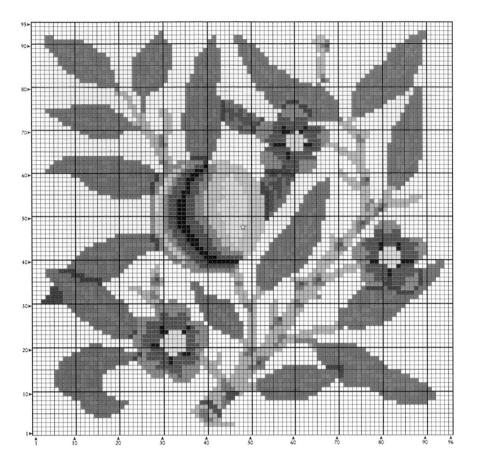

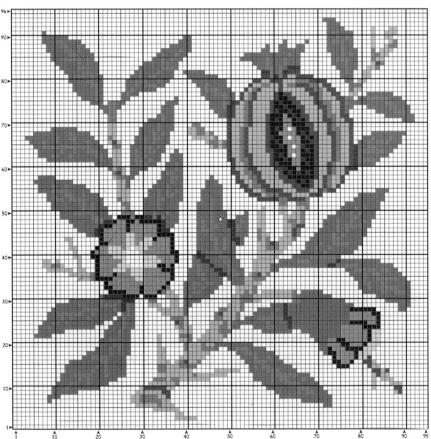

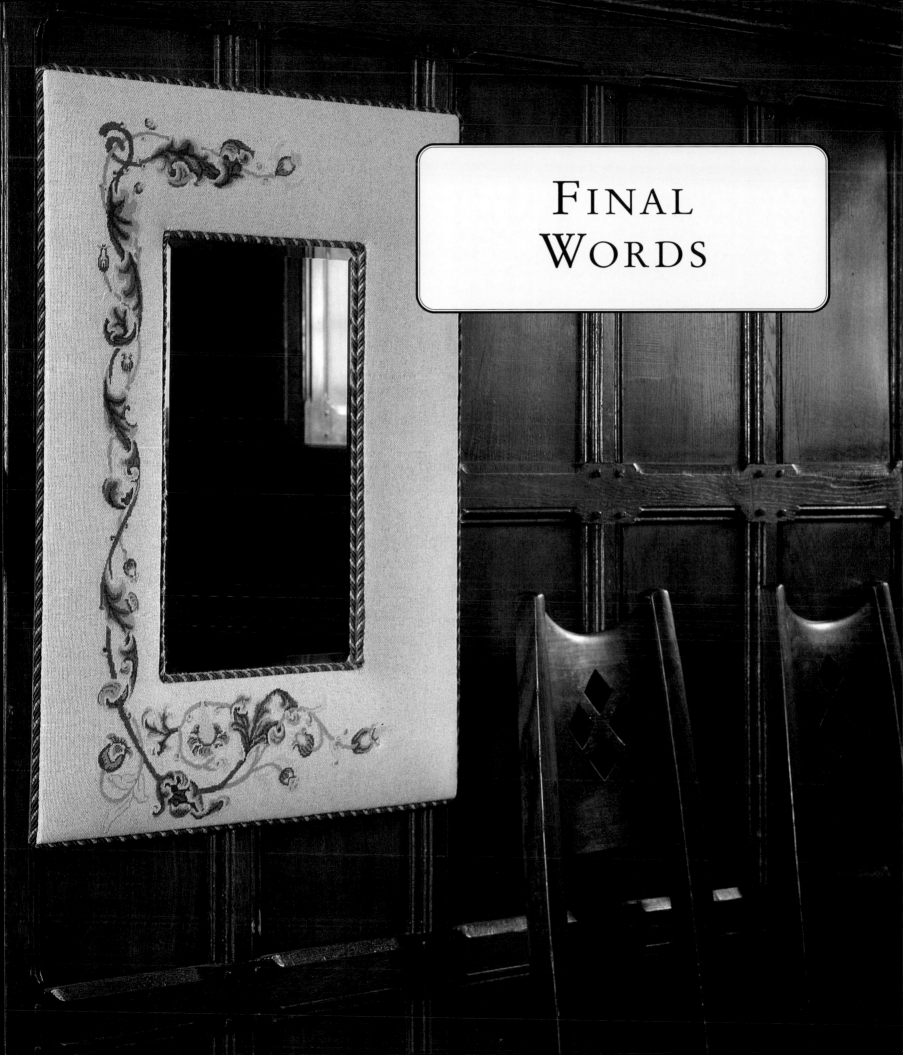

# FINAL
# WORDS

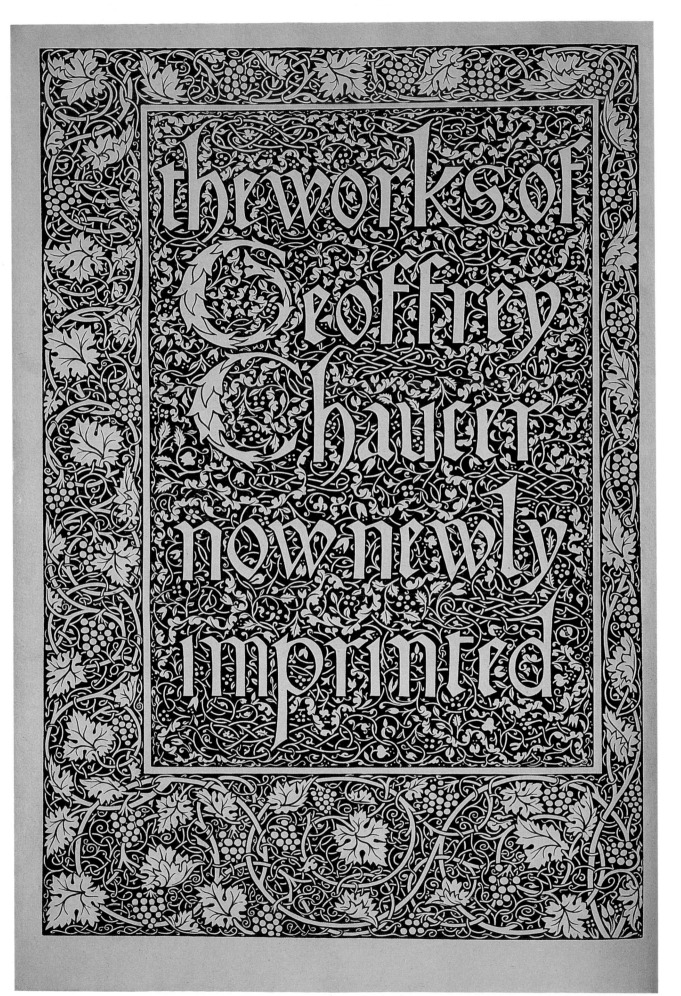

I do not want art for a few, any more than
education for a few, or freedom for a few

*The Lesser Arts, 1877*

IN THE SPRING of 1879, while Janey was in Italy, Morris found his last home. Kelmscott House, as it was to be renamed, looked over the same river that flowed near his beloved Kelmscott Manor. Morris liked the garden and the large room with long windows facing the Thames; he wrote to Janey describing it all. Rossetti had previously viewed the empty house and had also written to Janey secretly and disparagingly. She later said that she liked it more than she had expected. The William Morris Society is thankfully still housed in the basement, but it is a tragedy that we are unable to see the house as it was.

More than Red House, which was before the days of "The Firm," and more than Kelmscott Manor, this home was a perfect example of the use Morris made of all his furnishings. George Bernard Shaw – later to be romantically linked with May Morris – said that "there was an extraordinary discrimination at work in this magical house... everything that was necessary was clean and handsome and everything else was beautiful and beautifully presented." It was in his bedroom here that Morris wove his tapestry *Acanthus and Vine*.

In 1881, with his friend William De Morgan, Morris found the perfect site for Morris & Co. Merton Abbey was close to London and on the River Wandle, with dye vats already installed. At last, Morris had enough space for his needs –

A PAGE FROM THE KELMSCOTT *CHAUCER*. THIS PUBLICATION WAS THE CULMINATION OF A LIFE OF LEARNING AND STRIVING FOR PERFECTION BY MORRIS. IT MUST HAVE GIVEN HIM SUCH PLEASURE.

seven acres to house his fabric-printing, tapestry- and cloth-weaving, carpet-making, and stained glass production. He excitedly raised roofs and planted trees. The picture we have is a romantic one: "The room is full of sunlight and color. The upright frames face you at right angles with a long row of windows looking close upon the bright shining river." Outside, there were herbs, vegetables, and wild flowers growing and newly dyed fabrics spread out to dry in the sun.

Within three years there were one hundred employees, and Morris started designing wallpapers again. This was his most prolific period; he wrote: "I am drawing patterns so fast that last night I dreamed I had to draw a sausage; somehow I had to eat it first, which made me anxious about my digestion."

Secure in the financial success of his company, Morris devoted the next few years to the security of others. He worked incredibly hard for the Socialist

cause, writing, speaking, and marching; but he was bitterly disappointed by what he saw as his failure to make any appreciable difference to the standard of living of the working classes. He showed great courage and probably ruined his health.

His last and, to my mind, greatest achievement was the Kelmscott Press. Long an admirer of ancient illuminated manuscripts, Morris set about learning all aspects of book production, from paper-making to typography. His intention was to produce works of art. He designed three new typefaces and over 600 decorations. Twenty-three of his own titles were produced on the three handpresses in the little cottage near Kelmscott House. His masterpiece was the Kelmscott *Chaucer* – five years in the making. Morris received first copies of it just three months before he died. We can but wonder what he might have done next, had he lived longer.

William Morris died at Kelmscott House in October 1896; Janey, May, and Georgiana Burne-Jones were with him. A doctor at the time gave the cause of death as just being William Morris and doing the work of ten men.

His coffin was plain oak; he was taken by train through Oxford to Lechlade and from there in a moss-lined, yellow-painted haycart, decorated with vines and willows, through the rain to the pretty little church at Kelmscott.

Robert Blatchford wrote in *The Clarion* of 18th October, 1896:

*He was our best man. We cannot spare him; we cannot replace him. In all England there lives no braver, kinder, honester, cleverer, heartier man than William Morris. He is dead, and we cannot help feeling for a while that nothing else matters.*

THE FIRST PAGES OF MORRIS'S KELMSCOTT PRESS PUBLICATION OF *NEWS FROM NOWHERE* GIVE A FAIR INDICATION OF THE AMOUNT OF WORK MORRIS PUT INTO THE DESIGNING OF HIS LOVELY BOOKS. THE HOUSE SHOWN IS ACTUALLY KELMSCOTT MANOR.

# Kelmscott Frame

ON 26TH MAY, 1897, Edward Burne-Jones was heard to say: "There are two arts which others don't care for that Mr Morris and I have found our greatest delight in – painted books and beautiful tapestry."

The enormous enthusiasm that Morris displayed for everything he admired was particularly evident with books. His early love of literature developed into a passion for its decoration. He bought his first great book in 1864 at the age of 30; it was the 1473 Ulm edition of Boccaccio's *De Claris Mulieribus* and it cost £26. Twenty-eight years later he spent £900 on the *Tiptoft Missal*. At the time of his death he was considered an important collector, owning 800 early printed books and 100 illuminated manuscripts. Unfortunately, his collecting coincided with a drop in income and his slightly guilty need to justify his later acquisitions hugely amused his friends. When Morris stated that "prudence is a great mistake," Burne-Jones knew at once that his friend was about to purchase another medieval book!

In later life, Morris was to realize a dream. He produced his own writings on his own Kelmscott Press. Here, he controlled the size, the paper, the ink, the illustrations, and the type. He wanted to print books "that would have a definite claim to beauty." Just a glance at any one of the Kelmscott Press titles confirms that he certainly succeeded.

I was fortunate enough to read one of his romances, *The Well at the World's End*, in the original version. It was an absolute delight. It is not just the story that makes the turning of each page so compulsive; on each spread there is something new to charm. Single leaves and simple flowers punctuate Morris's own large and legible print. Beautiful illuminated letters start each section. A border might be filled with a tumble of grapes or a flourish of foliage. Although the influence of medieval manuscripts is obvious, each of the Kelmscott books is distinctly Morris's own creation.

The casual way a three-sided design in *The Well at the World's End* framed the page fascinated me. I so wanted to see if the black-and-white original would work in embroidery. It is an intricate design and even on fine linen I needed to enlarge it considerably to retain its marvelous flamboyance. Linen is ideal; its natural color looks beautiful on the unworked side of the frame and of course it negates the need for background stitching.

I am not as familiar with cotton threads as I am with Appleton wool yarns, and this unnerved me as I started my experimental stitching. Fortunately, this was when I was rescued by my son Nick's new computer program, which allowed me to match the threads that I had chosen and to "stitch" on the screen. It was so exciting watching my frame grow – I could go back and correct stitches without unpicking – what a joy!

There was a disadvantage to using so many stitches – the chart had to be printed in sixteen parts. It was with these stuck together in an unwieldy shape, along with the linen and the cotton threads, that I approached Angela Reader, who is an extremely experienced stitcher. Fortunately, she is not easily daunted, understood my explanation for the lopsided design and calmly matched the centers and started stitching. I do not think that I have ever seen one of my designs turn out so exactly as I had expected. The acanthus leaves especially pleased me, and Angela's stitching is smooth and even – much better than mine!

ABOVE A SUPERB EXAMPLE OF A 15TH-CENTURY GRADUAL FROM THE CATHEDRAL OF SIENA, WHICH MORRIS MIGHT HAVE STUDIED AND ADMIRED.

FAR LEFT MY KELMSCOTT FRAME ON MAHOGANY PANELING IN LIBERTY'S FURNITURE DEPARTMENT.

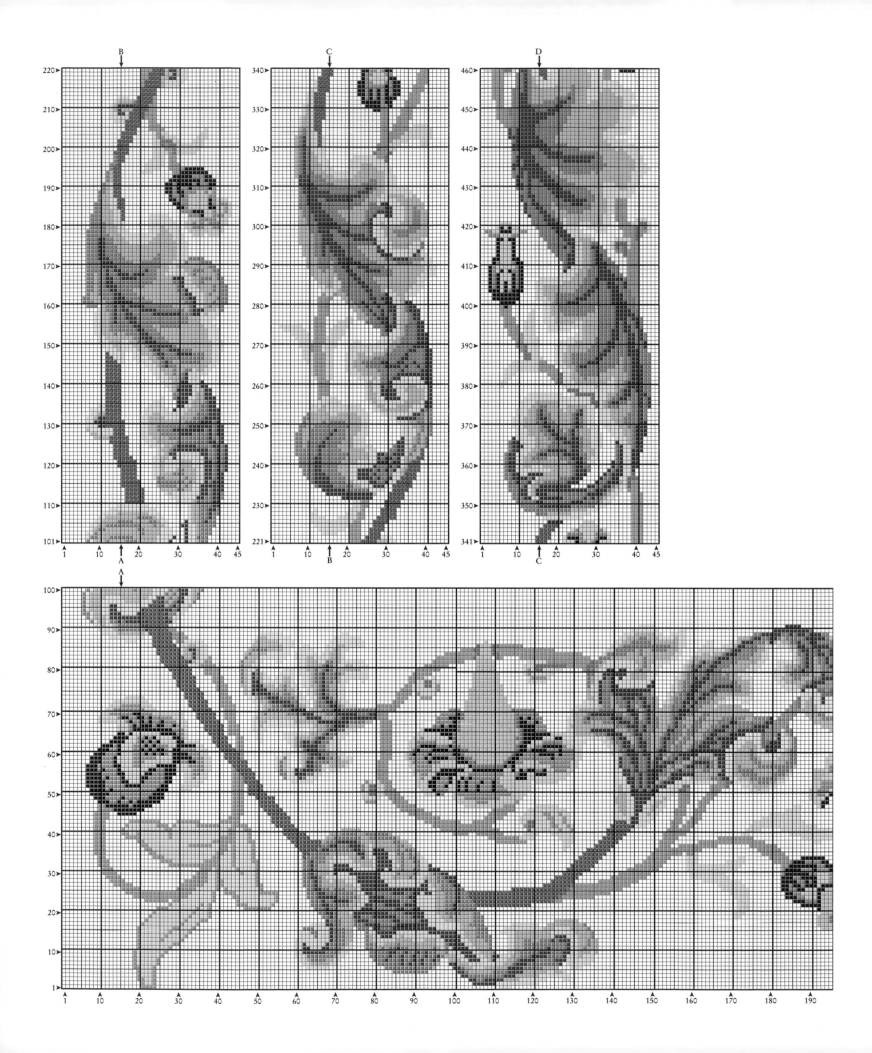

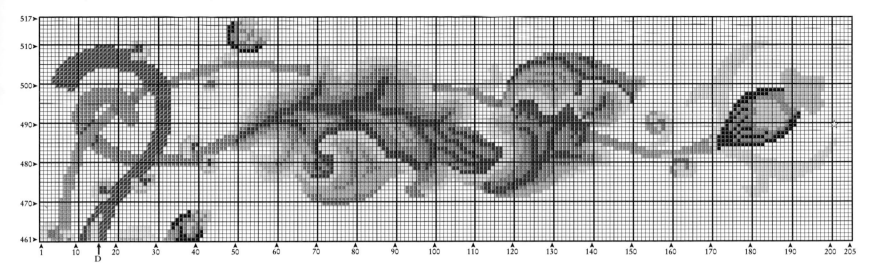

MATERIALS FOR THE KELMSCOTT FRAME

**Linen:** 18 threads/in (7/cm) evenweave linen
    measuring 40 x 33in (102 x 84cm)
**Threads:** DMC cotton embroidery floss
**Needle:** Size 24 tapestry
**Stitch:** Tent stitch, using 4 strands of floss
**Finished size of frame as shown:** 31¼ x 24½in
    (80 x 62cm); width 6½in (16.5cm)

The Kelmscott Frame was a tremendously satisfying project and I must confess to being slightly stunned by its elegance. I know it looks a little daunting, but I hope that you will not be frightened by it. If you plan carefully, all will be well. Perhaps you can take comfort in the fact that at least you can see how it will look when complete – I was not at all sure! If you like the design but have no need of a frame, you could use the chart to make a bell pull, curtain tie-back, or valance.

Check with your framer about fabric before you start. An extra 4in (10cm) of linen all around the frame gives you margin for error.

It is simpler to start at the top of the design. Stitch a guideline down the vertical center of your linen. Measure 7in (18cm) down from the top of the fabric along this line. Take this point as the intersection of 200 x 490 (see the ☆ in the chart above). Starting with the red-and-yellow flower and its leaf, work in tent stitch from right to left to the corner. Continue stitching down the side sections from D to C, C to B, and down to A at the bottom corner.

CHART AND COLOR KEY

The Kelmscott Frame was made
in DMC cotton floss.

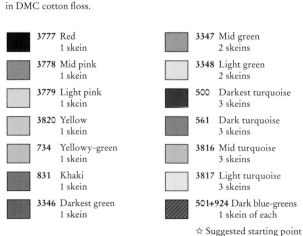

| | | | | |
|---|---|---|---|---|
| ■ | 3777 Red 1 skein | | | 3347 Mid green 2 skeins |
| | 3778 Mid pink 1 skein | | | 3348 Light green 2 skeins |
| | 3779 Light pink 1 skein | | ■ | 500 Darkest turquoise 3 skeins |
| | 3820 Yellow 1 skein | | ■ | 561 Dark turquoise 3 skeins |
| | 734 Yellowy-green 1 skein | | | 3816 Mid turquoise 3 skeins |
| | 831 Khaki 1 skein | | | 3817 Light turquoise 3 skeins |
| | 3346 Darkest green 1 skein | | | 501+924 Dark blue-greens 1 skein of each |

☆ Suggested starting point

ur that drave us awa...
r amidst of the hay,
ng was left us but one
biding that earth' way
illows comes up at the la...
llows ere autumn is past.

ain
ip from the main,
once more
ore,
e edge,
ge,
e bow,
e foe.

ath the mountain we came in the mor...
e fountain up over the corn,
s a/running fast on to the House
urs uncunning who quake at the mouse,
er is broken; they know not for why,
er was no token on earth or in sky.

up, then up!
board and cup,
ollow the gleam
ering stream
h the road
abode,
ed and white
on and the night;
w lies the neighbour that drave us away
h from his labour amidst of the hay.
he hills' brow is hiding the city undone,
for our riding is left us save one,
e house of the billows is with us at last,
e wind in the willows is done and o'er/past.

ASTE! mount and haste
Ere the short night waste,
For night and day,

Late turned away,
Draw nigh again
All kissing,/fain;
And the morn and the moon
Shall be married full soon.
So ride we together with wealth,/winning wand,
The steel o'er the leather, the ash in the hand,
Lo! white walls before us, and high are they built,
But the luck that outwore us now lies on their guilt
Lo! the open gate biding the first of the sun
And to peace are we riding when slaught...

WHEN Ralph had done singing, all folk fell to praising his song, whereas the Lord had praised the other one; but the Lord said, looking at Ralph ash- ance meanwhile: "Yea, if that pleaseth me not, & I take but little keep of it, it shall please my wife to her heart's root, & that is the first thing. Hast thou other good store, new— comer?" "Yea, lord," said Ralph. "And canst thou tell tales of yore agone, and of the fays & such/like? All that she must have," "Some deal I can of that lore," said Ralph. THEN the Lord sat si- lent, and seemed to be pondering: at last he said, as if to himself: "Yet there is one thing: many a blencher can sing of battle; & it hath been seen, that a fair body of a man is whiles soft amidst the hard hand,/play. Thou! Morfinn's luck! art thou of any use in the tilt,/yard?"

...thou
now go thou! D...
lad away to hi...
him a flask of...
to help out
with him"...
left the ter...
by David s...
ing head
he called...
ever bet...
as yet; ...t every day he was
drawing nigher to the Well at
the World's End; and that...
was most like that...
fall in with that...
his dream som...
way thereto. S...
head again, ...
himself as...
to enter...

# Grape

ABOVE DETAIL FROM A 16TH-CENTURY HOURS OF THE VIRGIN. LEFT MARKING THE PLACE THAT INSPIRED IT, MY GRAPE BOOKMARK ON MORRIS'S *THE WELL AT THE WORLD'S END*.

THE ILLUSTRATED BOOKS printed on the Kelmscott Press are a source of enormous pleasure to me. They were produced with a generosity of design detail that is just astonishing. The drawing on which I based my Grape bookmark is so understated on an inside margin that it could easily be overlooked.

I wanted to keep the bookmark as discreet as its original and so chose very fine linen and soft colors. The climbing stems were rather ambitious on the small size and I was ages getting the knot in the stem to look right. The original is in outline only and the single bunch of grapes is quite sufficient; in color, however, I felt that I needed a second splash of rich fruit to balance the design.

The Grape bookmark is another example of my computer-charting and has taught me a lesson. I can chart only a small section at a time and I did not study the joined chart closely enough to realize that Morris balanced the composition to lie straight along the text on the right-hand side. Given another chance, I might move the bottom stem over to the left, but it does not spoil it for me – just makes it more special.

MATERIALS FOR THE GRAPE BOOKMARK

**Linen:** 28 threads/in (11/cm) ivory evenweave linen measuring 13 x 5in (33 x 13cm)

**Threads:** DMC cotton embroidery floss

**Needle:** Size 26 tapestry

**Finished size of design:** 6¼ x 1in (16 x 2.5cm)

**Stitch:** Tent stitch, using 2 strands of cotton embroidery floss

**Size of bookmark including fringe:** 11 x 1½in (28 x 4cm)

For the model shown, the linen was folded back to form the lining. A three-sided stitch – a form of pulled thread work – was used for decoration, 12 threads above the design and 27 below. The fringe was made by pulling out the weft threads. A simple backstitch would be enough to hold the fringe, but you could have fun creating your own decoration.

There are a number of evenweave ribbons available both in linen and Aida. If you do not want to line the bookmark, a 1½in (4cm) wide band of 28 threads/in (11/cm) linen would be ideal. Both ends would need to be fringed and anchored and, naturally, the back of your work very neat!

Just to remind you that you need not simply copy my sample – on 8 threads/in (3/cm) canvas, this would make a bell pull nearly 2ft (60cm) long.

CHART AND COLOR KEY

The Grape bookmark was made in DMC cotton floss.

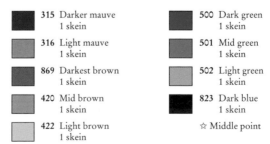

| | | | |
|---|---|---|---|
| 315 | Darker mauve 1 skein | 500 | Dark green 1 skein |
| 316 | Light mauve 1 skein | 501 | Mid green 1 skein |
| 869 | Darkest brown 1 skein | 502 | Light green 1 skein |
| 420 | Mid brown 1 skein | 823 | Dark blue 1 skein |
| 422 | Light brown 1 skein | ☆ | Middle point |

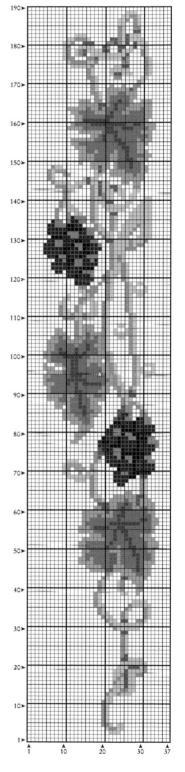

# Rose

ABOVE ROSE WORKED IN WOOLS AT A WINDOW AT RED HOUSE.
LEFT ROSE ON LINEN, COMPLEMENTING MORRIS'S KELMSCOTT
EDITION OF *THE WELL AT THE WORLD'S END*.

"THE DOUBLE ROSE WAS a gain to the world, a new beauty was given us by it." Morris had very strong opinions on flowers and a great knowledge of them; he loved roses and we see them frequently in his designs and writings.

My Rose bookmark is based on a decoration from Morris's Kelmscott edition of *The Well at the World's End*. Morris's rose is clearly a climber – the stem meanders down the edge of the page and across the foot to end in the pretty flower head. It seems appropriate that it should become a bookmark.

In order not to make my design too wide, I omitted one sprig of leaves. The bookmark worked on rough linen has a natural, down-to-earth look that I feel Morris would have liked, along with the old faded colors of the flower. I wanted to try the design again but without altering the size. So, I used canvas of the same gauge and stitched it in stronger colored wool yarns. By the time I had added Morris's favorite indigo-blue background and the silky fringe, it looked quite different.

## MATERIALS FOR THE CANVAS ROSE BOOKMARK

**Canvas:** 18 threads/in (7/cm) Zweigart mono canvas measuring 6 x 12½in (15 x 32cm)

**Threads:** Appleton crewel yarn

**Needle:** Size 22 tapestry

**Finished size of design:** 1½ x 7¼in (4 x 18.5cm)

**Stitch:** Tent stitch, using 2 strands of crewel yarn

### CHART AND COLOR KEY

The canvas Rose bookmark was made in Appleton crewel yarn.

- 757 Dark pink, 1 skein
- 944 Mid pink, 1 skein
- 942 Light pink, 1 skein
- 751 Pale pink, 1 skein
- 244 Dark green, 1 skein
- 543 Mid green, 1 skein
- 205+543 Browny-pink + Mid green, 1 skein of each
- 512 Light green, 1 skein
- 915 Brown, 1 skein
- 205+915 Browny-pink + Brown, 1 skein of each
- 926 Blue (background), 3 skeins
- ☆ Middle point

## MATERIALS FOR THE LINEN ROSE BOOKMARK

**Linen:** 18 threads/in (7/cm) evenweave linen measuring 6 x 14in (15 x 35.5cm)

**Threads:** DMC cotton embroidery floss

**Needle:** Size 22 tapestry

**Finished size of design:** 1½ x 7¼in (4 x 18.5cm)

**Stitch:** Tent stitch, using 4 strands of floss

### CHART AND COLOR KEY

The linen Rose bookmark was made in DMC cotton floss.

- 3726 Dark pink, 1 skein
- 3727 Mid pink, 1 skein
- 778 Light pink, 1 skein
- 819 Pale pink, 1 skein
- 937 Dark green, 1 skein
- 470 Mid green, 1 skein
- 356+470 Browny-pink + Mid green, 1 skein of each
- 3348 Light green, 1 skein
- 610 Brown, 1 skein
- 356+610 Browny-pink + Brown, 1 skein of each
- ☆ Middle point

# Tulip

MORRIS PRODUCED HIS fabric *Medway* during his extremely creative time at Merton Abbey. It is marvelous to know that after the immense effort he put into learning the art of natural dyeing it was all so productive. Originally *Medway* was shown with a blue ground and it would have required indigo, weld, and madder to achieve the blues, pinks, reds, and greens of that first printing.

The *Medway* design is unusual in that, as *Garden Tulip*, it was also used as a wallpaper design. Morris emphasized that designs meant to be viewed flat should be approached slightly differently from those that will naturally fall into folds. However, the dignified rows of curving stems in *Medway* would lend themselves to either treatment.

Along with the *Strawberry Thief* fabric from the same period, *Medway* was one of the first Morris designs that I was attracted to. It is so fine that I did not attempt it on canvas, but produced it as a transfer to use for free embroidery. I had always thought of it worked in silk threads as a border for curtains. It came to mind again recently and seemed quite perfect for my book cover. It does work in tent stitch and would also make a very pretty bell pull.

My cover is simply the height of the book with 3in (7.5cm) flaps to contain the covers. You may want to decorate the spine and back of the book, so plan the positioning of the design.

Line your completed linen with a fine fabric, fold back the flaps so that the book fits, and stitch top and bottom.

## MATERIALS FOR THE TULIP BOOK COVER

**Linen:** 18 threads/in (7/cm) natural evenweave linen
**Threads:** DMC cotton embroidery floss
**Needle:** Size 22 tapestry
**Finished size of design area:** 7½ x 9¼in (19 x 23.5cm)
**Stitch:** Tent stitch, using 4 strands of floss

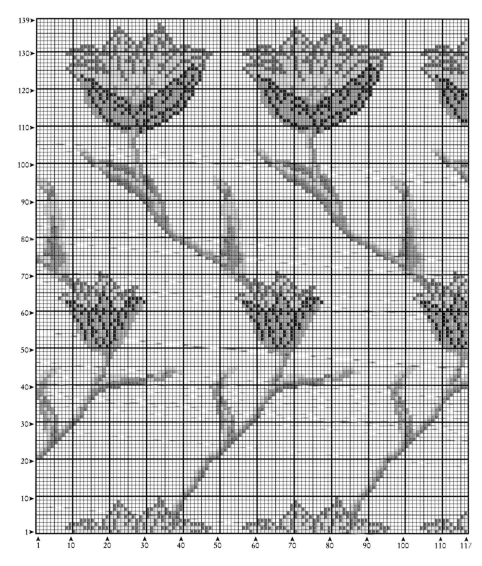

**CHART AND COLOR KEY**

The Tulip book cover was made in DMC cotton floss.

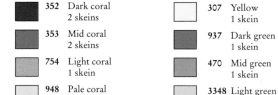

| | | |
|---|---|---|
| 352 | Dark coral | 2 skeins |
| 353 | Mid coral | 2 skeins |
| 754 | Light coral | 1 skein |
| 948 | Pale coral | 1 skein |
| 307 | Yellow | 1 skein |
| 937 | Dark green | 1 skein |
| 470 | Mid green | 1 skein |
| 3348 | Light green | 1 skein |

FAR LEFT TULIP decorating my ROYAL HORTICULUTRAL SOCIETY diary and my experimental stitching for an evening purse on an antique frame.

# Acanthus & Flower

ALL THE DECORATED BOOKS from the Kelmscott Press offer a wealth of design ideas. I longed to adapt the extremely elaborate borders that frame the romantic Burne-Jones drawings. I thoroughly enjoyed myself drawing and coloring the intertwining stems and curled petals and leaves. It is so important that the lines curve evenly and that the design makes sense, and it is not until I have colored the design or stitched it that I can tell if it is possible to follow the path of a stem as it winds over and under others.

With great reluctance I conceded that to use the whole intricate page was impractical and instead took just a lovely detail. It is significant that this part of the design works well on its own. The sweep of the acanthus leaves is such a distinctive Morris flourish – almost a signature.

This is an extremely adaptable design. I should like to see it on a delicate workbox, or it would make a stylish cover for an address book or diary. Do remember that if it is worked in tent stitch on this gauge of linen it will be half the size. It would make a hardy stool cover if stitched in wool yarns on canvas with the background worked.

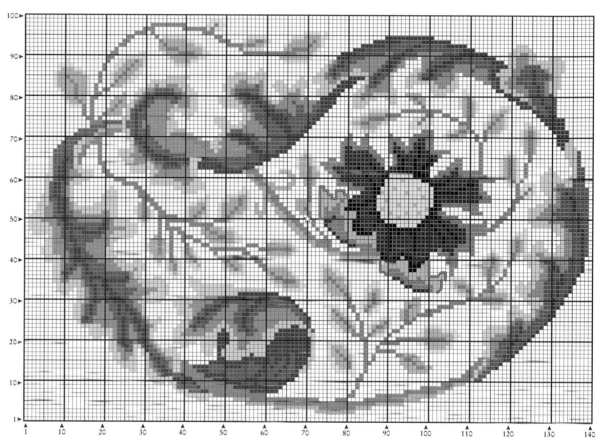

### MATERIALS FOR THE ACANTHUS & FLOWER FOOTSTOOL

**Linen:** 28 threads/in (11/cm) evenweave linen
**Threads:** DMC cotton embroidery floss
**Needle:** Size 26 tapestry
**Finished size of design area:** 10¼ x 7¼in (26 x 18.5cm)
**Stitch:** Cross stitch, over 2 fabric threads, using 2 strands of floss

CHART AND COLOR KEY

The Acanthus & Flower footstool was made in DMC cotton floss.

| | | | | |
|---|---|---|---|---|
| 3721 | Dark pink 1 skein | | 937 | Dark green 1 skein |
| 223 | Mid pink 1 skein | | 470 | Mid green 1 skein |
| 224 | Light pink 1 skein | | 3348 | Light green 1 skein |
| 225 | Pastel pink 1 skein | | 500 | Dark blue-green 2 skeins |
| 833 | Yellow 1 skein | | 930 | Darkest marine blue 2 skeins |
| 3011 | Dark olive green 1 skein | | 931 | Mid marine blue 2 skeins |
| 3012 | Mid olive green 1 skein | | 932 | Light marine blue 2 skeins |
| 3013 | Pale olive green 1 skein | | ☆ | Middle point |

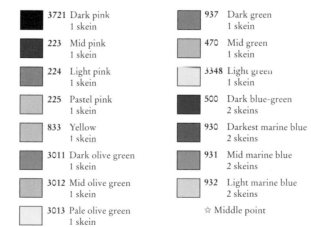

FAR LEFT ACANTHUS & FLOWER ON A BEDROOM FOOTSTOOL NESTLING AMONG THE SPRING BLUEBELLS IN AN ENGLISH GARDEN.

# Basic Techniques

I can never be contented with getting anything short of the best,

and I shall always go on trying to improve our goods in all ways,

and should consider anything that was only tolerable as a ladder

to mount up to the next stage – that is, in fact, my life.

WILLIAM MORRIS TO THOMAS WARDLE, 1876

MY SINCERE HOPE is that you will use this book as Morris would have wished – as a starting point for your own journey into this important art of embroidery.

Morris devoted his life to the betterment of others by showing us how to search for our own creativity. It seems churlish of us not to pay attention, and I think that when we do listen and eventually lose ourselves in our own projects, we will find that he has pinpointed the essence of happiness.

Needlepoint is the easiest embroidery technique. Most of the projects in this book have been made using one simple stitch. The creativity comes with the choosing of the colors and materials. It is color that I find most fascinating, and usually it is on the color that I spend most time, trying to get it absolutely right. I have never quite succeeded, so I persuade myself that it is the journey rather than the arrival that is more pleasant; I do love the experimental stages at the start of a new project.

Once a few minutes have been spent mastering the techniques of tent stitch and the purpose of charts, then, with materials

PEACOCK HANGING IN THE VAULTED PASSAGE AT BROUGHTON CASTLE, OXFORDSHIRE.

at hand, you can launch into your first piece. However, the following golden rules might help you to avoid a few irritating pitfalls.

1 Only start something you love. Stitching is time-consuming and this time should be hugely enjoyable. I want you to experience the warm security of happy dreams each time you pick up your work. If you do, then you will finish your pieces and have the bonus of seeing them – as Morris advocated – forming part of your home as something beautiful and perhaps useful.

2 Think carefully about the size of your chosen design, and work out what gauge of fabric you will need. Some people are happiest producing marvelous miniatures with the tiniest of stitches, but if your idea of bliss is an easily seen 12 threads to the inch canvas and one thread of tapestry yarn, it is vital that this is what you choose, even if you need to adapt the design.

3 Make absolutely sure that the fabric you are going to stitch is large enough for the final product. With canvaswork you should have at least 2in (5cm) of unworked canvas all around the finished stitching. For awkward shapes, such as chairs or frames, it might be wiser to make a template or discuss your ideas with your upholsterer

or framer before you start. Then make sure that you position the design accurately on the fabric, not necessarily in the center.

4 If the colors and threads are going to vary from those I have specified, it makes sound sense to experiment with yours by stitching on scraps of fabric or canvas to make sure you are happy with the way the colors affect each other. I never produce a design unless I have done this.

## CHARTS

My designs are meant to whet your appetite. As in cooking, it is always easier to adapt a recipe than to start from scratch. The charts are recipes – infinitely adaptable. They give you enormous freedom. You are free to choose the size of your project, the type and gauge of your evenweave fabric, the sort of threads, and the colors.

The charts show clearly the number of shades required to make any given shape in the design. There is nothing to prevent the adventurous stitcher from changing the color of these shades entirely – green leaves can become brown... spring changes to autumn as you stitch.

I have tried to show some of the different effects you can achieve with a chart. We can see that all the Border cushions will make fabulous rugs, and how magnificent the Peacock looks as a huge wall hanging! It is not hard to imagine Vine and Apples as chair seats; you may need more or fewer leaves or fruit to fit your chair, but all the elements are in the charts; it is just a matter of placing them differently. You can also use single elements of a chart – just a leaf or a flower, whatever you need.

The chart tells you the number of stitches you need to make that design, or part of the design, and it is this that allows you to calculate the gauge and size of canvas or fabric you will need to work on. Each square on the chart represents one stitch.

## EVENWEAVE FABRICS

Your ability to transfer a charted design onto fabric depends entirely on that fabric having an even weave – this means that the threads are evenly spaced both vertically and horizontally and that the number of threads within a given distance are the same. If you have an evenweave fabric that is said to be 18 gauge, it means that within an inch you can count 18 fabric threads. Without this even weave, the stitches will not be spaced evenly and so the design will not look as it does on the chart.

### Canvas

For me, the most pleasant evenweave fabric to use is Zweigart's deluxe mono canvas. It has smooth, polished threads, and its quality and strength are superior to those of other makes of canvas. Unfortunately, but understandably, it is more expensive. Zweigart have been producing embroidery fabrics since 1877, when Morris was in full flow, and their insistence on quality is similar to his. It is essential that your precious time is spent working with the best materials.

Canvas is made in several different ways. The deluxe mono that I prefer is woven in the traditional way with the threads held in place only by the tension of the weaving and the selvages at the sides. You can find it in gauges from 18 to 10 threads to the inch (7 to 4 threads to the centimeter).

Double canvas has two threads traveling together for each one of mono canvas. This is useful for petit point and gros point on the same canvas, and it can be trammed. As it is not so easily counted as mono canvas, I feel it is less suited to charted designs.

With interlock canvas, the threads are not woven over and under as in mono canvas, but interlocked at each intersection so that they cannot be moved toward each other. In finer gauges of interlock canvas, the threads tend to be much thinner than in mono canvas and it feels very soft initially. As it is inclined to tear if much stretching is needed, I would advise using it only for tiny pieces or if you need something very pliable. However, Zweigart's interlock rug canvas – from 8 to 4½ threads/in (3 to 2 threads/cm) – is very strong and ideally suited to cross stitch.

### Linen

Wherever I have used canvas in this book, you can substitute linen, and vice versa. Evenweave linen comes in fine gauges – most usually 18 threads/in (7 threads/cm), 28/in (11/cm) and 32/in (12.5/cm).

The background is usually left unworked on linen, so you must finish off your ends neatly and not allow threads to loop from one group of stitches to another, as these will show through on the front of the work.

## GAUGE

This means the number of threads to the inch measured across the canvas. The more threads the "finer" the canvas.

When you consider that each fabric thread requires a stitch, it follows that the finer the canvas or linen, the greater the number of stitches needed to cover a comparable area. You can work out the eventual size of a stitched piece if you know the number of stitches in the design and the gauge of the canvas. If the design needs 96 stitches and your canvas has 12 threads/in, the stitched piece will measure 8in (20cm). If you want it larger, use a coarser fabric, one with fewer threads to the inch; 96 stitches on a canvas with 10 threads/in (4 threads/cm) will produce a design of just over 9½in (24cm).

An important point to remember with linen – or any evenweave fabric – is that cross stitch is normally worked over two fabric threads and so takes up twice as much space. A 28 threads/in linen that is worked in cross stitch will produce a design the same size as one worked in tent stitch on 14 threads/in canvas.

## THREADS

### Wool yarns

Appleton yarns are my favorite. Appleton is the only manufacturer that provides up to nine shades in any one color. For instance, there are eight different "families" of green and each one ranges from five to nine shades. For complex shapes it is lovely to have the luxury of such a choice.

Appleton tapestry yarn is equivalent to three strands of their crewel yarn, in spite of the fact that crewel yarn is 2 ply and tapestry 4 ply; all 417 Appleton colors are available in either. I "think" my designs in Appleton and have great difficulty visualizing the effect of other threads.

For most stitchers, tapestry yarn is suitable for tent stitch on 12 or 14 threads/in canvas. However, sometimes tapestry is too thick on 14 gauge, so I would recommend crewel yarn for this gauge, which gives you the option of using two threads for the design and three for the background. Mixing tapestry and crewel on the same canvas does not matter; many of my original samples have been stitched using both and it is impossible to see the difference. You can also blend colors in the needle with crewel yarn. The colors fall quite randomly and give the effect of another shade.

Appleton yarns are sold in hanks of approximately 25g or just under an ounce (about 208yd/190m crewel and 61yd/56m tapestry) or skeins (about 27yd/25m crewel and 11yd/10m tapestry). The hanks look like the old knitting yarn we had to hold for our mothers to wind. If you cut the looped hank at either end, you will have lengths of thread 30in (76cm) long. It is easy to pull off a few strands of crewel from a cut hank and thread them together. I find this an ideal length, although some will consider it too long, especially if using a rougher canvas which might wear the yarn faster. This is why I always prefer to use the polished canvas. But as I have said before, it is always better to do what pleases you and what you find works well.

**Cotton floss**

I have used DMC cotton floss for my designs on linen. They are sold in 8m (8¾yd) skeins consisting of 6 strands of floss. You will need a different number of strands for different gauges of fabric.

It is wise to separate each strand before threading them to help them to lie flat. Twisted strands do not have quite the sheen of flat ones.

## NEEDLES

Your needle needs to pass between the fabric threads without piercing them or the

The linen cross stitch version of Lemon on a workbox.

embroidery thread, so a sharp needle is a disadvantage. Tapestry needles are blunt-ended and have easily threaded long eyes.

## FRAMES

"To frame or not to frame" is probably the question I am most often asked. As with all else, it is no one's decision but yours, but I strongly advocate it for all work on soft fabrics such as linen. For canvaswork it will help keep the canvas straight and taut but it will not necessarily cancel the need for stretching. The most important advantage is that it allows the use of two hands, one above and one below the work, passing the needle from one to another.

The disadvantages are the bother of putting the work on the frame in the first place and the fact that it is slightly less portable; it is also impossible to "scoop" the stitches, that is taking the needle in and out in one movement, which I know many stitchers enjoy doing.

## STITCHING

To start stitching, make a knot in the thread (or threads) and, choosing a part of the design you are about to work toward, take the needle down from above the fabric about 1-1½in (2.5-4cm) from your starting place, leaving the knot on the top side. Bring the needle up where you intend to start stitching. As you stitch toward the knot, the thread at the back becomes woven in and thus secured. Cut off the knot when you reach it with the stitching. Similarly, you can finish off by bringing the thread to the top an inch or so from where you are working, so that it will be secured later. This means that you do not have to turn the work over to finish off – a big advantage if you are working on a large frame. Alternatively, thread the end through some stitches at the back of your work.

**Tent stitch**

Tent stitch was used for the majority of projects in this book. It is a stitch that comes quite naturally, not unlike hemming a skirt. It can be worked on a frame or in the hand. It is, however, a diagonal stitch and, as such, is somewhat of a nuisance as it tends to pull the canvas out of shape. Tent stitch can be worked in horizontal, vertical or diagonal rows. The basketweave form of tent stitch is worked in diagonal rows and distorts the canvas less than the other two methods. One tent stitch is equivalent to one square on the charts.

I advocate tent stitch as it is small, can depict detail and is hard wearing. It forms a long, diagonal stitch on the back of the work, traveling under two fabric threads, thereby anchoring them.

There is another small, diagonal stitch called half-cross stitch which looks exactly the same as tent stitch on the front of the needlepoint. However, it is unsuitable for mono canvas or evenweave linen as it forms a short, straight stitch on the back that can, if pulled, slip between the fabric threads if they are not interlocked.

**Cross stitch**

This usually consists of two half-cross stitches lying in opposite directions, one on top of the other. If these are made over one thread of the fabric, the fabric needs to be interlocked to prevent the stitches sliding between the fabric threads. Alternatively, the stitches must be made over two threads of the fabric.

I always advocate cross stitch for rugs as it pulls evenly in each direction which helps the finished piece to retain its shape. It is a hard-wearing stitch because of the double thickness of the thread. As rug canvas is almost always interlocked, each stitch need only be made over one canvas thread. In contrast, the cross stitch on the Acanthus & Flower footstool on page 114 and the Lemon workbox top on page 119 is worked over two linen threads. On linen, cross stitch has to be worked over two fabric threads.

In theory, cross stitch can just as well be formed with two tent stitches lying one over the other, or even with one half-cross stitch and one tent stitch. All would look the same on the front of the needlepoint, but the latter would not pull as evenly. It is important to keep all the top stitches lying in the same direction for a neat finish. Remember when you are calculating sizes that cross stitch over two threads of fabric rather than one will double the stitched area. One cross stitch is the equivalent of one square on the charts.

**Florentine stitch**

This is a refreshingly simple, straight stitch which does not distort the canvas and is often worked over several canvas threads, thereby covering an area quite quickly. It does not, however, cover the canvas as efficiently as tent stitch and one extra strand of crewel yarn is needed for it (possibly more). Do try it out for yourself before getting too far into your project.

There are many excellent books devoted to the various needlepoint stitches and it can be enormous fun to experiment not just with your background stitch but also the texture of different parts of the design.

## PREPARING FOR WORK

Now that you have your fabric, threads, chart, needle, scissors, frame (if needed), and good light, make any necessary markings on the canvas or linen. Use a waterproof pen if it is to be stitched over with a darker color, or brightly colored sewing thread. Now is the time to indicate the outline of a template and the middle point. Some people like to "quarter" the design by stitching along the center lines vertically and horizontally. Anything that will help you relate to the right square on the chart is a good idea.

Framing comes next. If you are not using one, then you may like to hem around your fabric to protect it from unraveling or catching the embroidery threads. You can also put masking tape around canvas or overcast linen edges. The canvas will need to be hemmed at a later stage to enable you to "stretch" it back to shape.

It is a good idea to sort your threads in daylight. I frequently use colors that are very close to one another and they alter in their relationships as different light falls on them. You need to be able to recognize them in any light so that you do not spend your evening stitching with a color that you had not intended to use. Put them in separate bundles, or label them. Now you are ready to go – enjoy yourself.

## FINISHING

This is a part of the creative process that I can do without! At this stage my enthusiasm wanes and I usually delegate to experts. But if you want to see the whole project through and promise not to get disheartened with stitching, here are some tips.

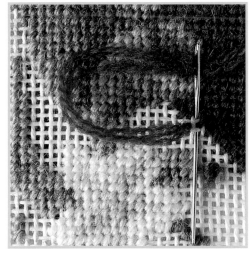

## TENT STITCH

*Top* This form of tent stitch is called continental. The needle passes behind two canvas threads and a long stitch forms on the back of the canvas. This gives the work a hard-wearing, padded back. If you use a frame, the needle passes down and then up in two separate movements.

*Above* For the next line of stitching, the needle travels in the opposite direction. If you are "scooping" your stitches, as here, you cannot use a frame and you will probably have rotated the canvas so that you can continue to stitch with your right hand traveling from right to left.

## BASKETWEAVE

*This form of tent stitch is used most often for backgrounds. This background was started by a single stitch in the top right-hand corner.*

*Top* The descending row. The needle is vertical and passes behind two canvas threads.

*Above* On the next ascending row, the needle is horizontal and still passing behind two canvas threads. Work the rows alternately to create the basketweave effect on the back. Two successive rows in one direction will show as a ridge on the front of the work. The knot used to start the work is cut off once the thread end is secured.

## CROSS STITCH

*Top* This first row is actually half-cross stitch – the needle is passing behind only one canvas thread and although the front looks like tent stitch, the back will not.

*Above* The crosses are completed with the needle still vertical. The back will show small, straight stitches. This is the same cross stitch as that used on linen, but as linen is not interlocked, the cross stitch must be made over two intersections of the linen.

*Some people prefer to complete each cross as they go.*

## Stretching

The finishing off of your stitched linen should require no more than a gentle press with an iron and a damp cloth on the back of the work. If it is slightly out of shape, pin it out on a board before pressing, but nothing drastic should be necessary.

Canvaswork is slightly different. With all the diagonal stitches of both the design and the background it is extremely rare that things do not get somewhat out of shape. Occasionally it can be only an inch out, but I think that it is worthwhile – after all your efforts – getting it perfect. I also think that it is worth having the stretching done professionally. It is normally not very expensive and not only does the canvas then become square again, but the stitches seem crisper. Choose your stretcher with care, however – ask how it is done and if possible look at already finished work.

If you want to do the stretching yourself, first hem around the raw canvas to make firm edges – this is why we allow 2in (5cm) all around the stitched area. Find a clean board larger than the canvas and rust-proof tacks or small nails. Using a large draftsman's triangle, nail the canvas right side down onto the board. I start in the center of one side and place a nail there; then, pulling the canvas, I add nails all along the hem to one corner at 1in (2.5cm) intervals, seeing that the worked edge of the canvas is straight. I then complete that side from the center to the other corner.

Now you will see if the canvas moves into the center away from the right angle or away from the center. I always tack the edge moving into the center next, pulling the canvas away from the corner, making the right angle and tacking all down that side – and so on across the bottom and up the other side. Each corner must be at right angles and each side straight. The canvas must be stretched, otherwise it will bubble in the middle and you will have to do it again. You can straighten the sides more efficiently by adding tacks between those already there. I usually spray on water after finishing the tacking, but if the canvas is badly out of shape, you might need to soften it by spraying after the first two sides are done.

I do not consider stretching an easy or a pleasant job, but it is worthwhile and necessary for almost all canvaswork. Even a chair seat, which is after all going to be stretched over the chair, will benefit from being made to look crisp beforehand. By using cross stitch, rugs will hopefully not get out of shape, but if they do the same rules apply. You just need an extremely big board – or you can have it done by experts.

## Cushions

All the cushions in this book have been backed with heavy upholstery cottons and decorated with cord. Even though I enthusiastically pass the cushion-making to my patient friend Dorothy Vernon, I do enjoy searching for cords and fabrics. When I fail totally to find a cord, Dorothy twists the Appleton yarns into one cord, using continuous lengths of whole hanks. The Fruit cushions were great fun as I found several fabrics that looked marvelous and I especially want to try a soft yellow backing for the Lemon and Orange. There are many embroidery shops that will stretch and make up your cushions, and twist the wool cord, if you wish.

Backing fabric should be 2in (5cm) larger than the stitched piece. Cord needs to be twice the width and height of the cushion, plus ½yd (50cm) for knots. The pillow form should be 10 per cent larger than the cushion cover.

Trim your canvas so that there is 1in (2.5cm) unworked all around. With canvas and fabric right sides together, pin and baste around three sides and four corners, extending for a short distance into the fourth side, following the edge of the needlepoint closely. Machine or hand stitch following your basting – you do not want any unworked canvas to show on your cushion. Pay particular attention to the corners; for them to be sharp and not pull out, the stitching must be firm. Fold back the raw edges of the canvas, mitering the corners, and lightly hand stitch them to the work so that they lie flat. Turn the cushion cover right side out and hand stitch the cord along the seam, knotting at the corners if you wish. For an invisible join, the ends of the cord should be spliced together. Place the pillow form in the cover and slip stitch together the last side.

I know that splicing the cord is not easy, so you can choose between tucking both ends in at the bottom of the cushion or, by not completing the fourth corner at the same time as the others, you can disguise the join behind a corner knot.

For each Fruit cushion, enough fabric was bought for both the backs and fronts. With the 1in (2.5cm) raw edges turned under, the canvases were positioned carefully on one side, hand sewn in place, and a fine cord was stitched all around before the cushions were finished with a heavier cord. The overall size of the smaller cushions is 14 x 14in (35.5 x 35.5cm); the larger cushion 14½ x 22½in (37 x 57cm). I chose the three leaf colors for the cords – 294, 296, and 241 for the Orange and Lemon cushions, 294, 296, and 911 for the Peach and Pomegranate cushions. You do need whole hanks of yarn to make the twisted cords.

## Rugs

If you can get your rug stretched, it will look crisper and, of course, it is important if it is out of shape. However, I do think that the soft look achieved at the end of all that stitching has its own appeal. Recently I have had a slight change of heart about backing rugs. A friend who collects valuable antique carpets pointed out that even the most fragile silk ones had no backing for fear of trapping dirt between the backing and the rug, which he said would cause wear. Now I am at a loss as to what to advise. I know of many of my rugs that have been beautifully backed and have already given years of wear. Perhaps one might feel slightly more secure with the back protected. If you decide you would like to try it, use a thin but firm, good quality felt for interlining and a stronger outer lining, such as burlap or holland.

## Hangings

The concept of covering our walls with embroidered fabric is very appealing. How the hanging should be attached depends largely on its size and, of course, on the height of the wall. The very large Peacock hanging, shown on page 19, has five loops made of 2½in (6cm) fabric tape. The loops needed to be large enough for the pole and they were hand sewn securely to the back of the work. The loops could have been made of canvas and stitched with the background color. It would be preferable to slip stitch a lining over the back of this to give it a nice finish – unless you think friends might feel deprived if they cannot sneak a peep at the back of your work!

For the smaller Peacock hanging, shown on page 116, the backing fabric has been used to make the loops and for its own lining. The border around the stitched piece is 3in (7.5cm) and the folded loops measure 3 x 3in (7.5 x 7.5cm). The canvas was hand stitched onto the front of the heavy cotton backing fabric and finished off with the Appleton wool cord before the lining was stitched in place.

## Kelmscott Frame

This really is a job for an expert, who should be consulted before you buy your fabric.

On 18 threads/in linen the width of the top and side stitching is 2½in (6.5cm) and that on the base just over 5in (13cm). The frame measures 6½in (16.5cm). It might look interesting if the sides and top of the frame were narrower than the base – see the illustration on page 49, where the border frames the tree in this way. Like many lovely antique embroidered frames, mine is slightly padded.

The instructions for the Frame tell you to start stitching as if the red-and-yellow flower at the top is just to the left of center. You may decide that you like the center an inch to the left. The extra 4in (10cm) of fabric for turnings allows you to delay this decision until stitching is complete.

The Ladies' Work Society, who made up my frame, prefers to add the cord around the beveled mirror and frame. Your framer may not. Our cord matched the design colors perfectly, but a natural linen-colored one to match the fabric would look equally good.

## Fire screens

Most fire screens are mounted in the same way as oil paintings within a frame. My Vine fire screen was easy to mount; the embroidery is suspended between two metal bars supported by four rings at the back.

## Chair seats and stools

It is worth going to a good upholsterer and asking for a template to be made before you start to make up a chair seat or stool. However, I have learned, to my cost, that it

ORANGE BORDER CUSHION IN THE GARDENS OF BROUGHTON CASTLE, OXFORDSHIRE.

is also worth checking that the upholsterer is familiar with needlepoint and understands that adjustments cannot be made once the stitching is complete. You do not want the odd quarter inch chopped off your work because the template did not fit!

Before framing your canvas or stitching, pin the template on the canvas. Ensure that you have at least 2in (5cm) of canvas outside the template and that the centre vertical line of the template runs straight along a thread. Mark the outline of the template; if the background is to be dark, you can use a waterproof pen, otherwise basting stitches are safer. Note and mark where you want the center of the design to fall. The canvas must not be cut until the stitching and stretching are complete.

## Bookmarks

The Rose design on linen has two rows of hem stitch worked in one of the pinks to finish it off. The canvas version is lined with silk and fringed with pearl cotton.

## BETH RUSSELL KITS

The Peacock, Raven, Lion, African Marigold, Orange Border, Artichoke I and II, Lemon, Orange, Peach, and Pomegranate designs are also produced as complete needlepoint kits in the collection of over 50 designs that I have adapted from William Morris and the Arts & Crafts Movement. The kits are *hand printed in full color* on deluxe mono Zweigart canvas and come complete with Appleton yarns, needle, detailed instructions, and a useful calico "wool-tidy" bag. They are available from many needlepoint stores. For further information regarding availability in the US, contact: **Potpourri Etc**, 209 Richmond Street, El Segundo, California 90245.
Tel: (310) 322 8512. Fax: (310) 322 0187.
Or drop me a line at **Designers Forum**, PO Box 565, London SW1V 3PU, England.

## APPLETON RETAILERS

Appleton yarns are available in many retail outlets throughout the US and Canada. The following are a few selected retailers and distributors. Further information about availability can be obtained from the Appleton head office in the UK:
**Appleton Bros Ltd,** Thames Works, Church Street, Chiswick, London W4 2PE, England.
Tel: (181) 994 0711. Fax: (181) 995 6609.

## USA
### ALABAMA
**Patches & Stitches**, 817A Regal Drive, Huntsville, Alabama 35801. Tel: (205) 533 3886.
**Sally S. Boom**, Wildwood Studio, PO Box 303, Montrose, Alabama 36559
Tel: (334) 928 1415.

### CALIFORNIA
**Fleur de Paris**, 5835 Washington Boulevard, Culver City, California 90230.
Tel: (213) 857 0704.

**Handcraft from Europe**, 1201-A Bridgeway, Sausalito, California 94965.
Tel: (415) 332 1633. Fax: (415) 334 5074.
**Natalie**, 144 North Larchmont Boulevard, Los Angeles, California 90004-3705.
Tel: (213) 462 2433.
**Needlepoint Inc**, 251 Post Street, 2nd Floor, San Francisco, California 94108.
Tel: (415) 392 1622.
**Rose Cottage**, 209 Richmond Street, El Segundo, California 90245.
Tel: (310) 322 8512. Fax: (310) 322 0187.

### DELAWARE
**The Jolly Needlewoman**, 5810 Kennett Pike, Centreville, Delaware 19807.
Tel: (302) 658 9585.

### LOUISIANA
**Needle Arts Studio**, 115 Metairie Road, Metairie, Louisiana 70005.
Tel: (504) 832 3050.

### MARYLAND
**The Elegant Needle**, 7945 MacArthur Boulevard, Suite 203, Cabin John, Maryland 20818.
Tel: (301) 320 0066.

### MASSACHUSETTS
**Stitches of the Past**, 68 Park Street, Andover, Massachusetts 01810.
Tel: (508) 475 3968. Fax: (508) 683 3146.

### MISSOURI
**Sign of the Arrow – 1867 Foundation Inc,** 9740 Clayton Road, St Louis, Missouri 63124.
Tel: (314) 994 0606.

### OHIO
**Louise's Needlework**, 45 North High Street, Dublin, Ohio 43017.
Tel: (614) 792 3505.

### PENNSYLVANIA
**Ewe And I**, 24 North Merion Avenue, Bryn Mawr, Pennsylvania 19010.
Tel: (610) 525 3028.

### TEXAS
**Access Commodities (L. Haidar),** PO Box 1778, Rockwall, Texas 75087.
Tel: (214) 722 1211. Fax: (214) 722 1302.
**Chaparral**, 3701 West Alabama, Suite 370, Houston, Texas 77027.
Tel: (713) 621 7562.
**Dan's Fifth Avenue**, 307 21st Street, Canyon, Texas 79015.
Tel: (806) 655 3355.

## CANADA
**Dick and Jane**, 2352 West 41st Avenue, Vancouver, British Columbia V6M 2A4.
Tel: (604) 738 3574.
**Fancyworks**, 110-3960 Quadra Street, Victoria, British Columbia V8X 4A3.
Tel: (604) 727 2765.
**Jet Handcraft Studio Ltd**, PO Box 91103, 225 17th Street, West Vancouver, British Columbia V7V 3N3.
Tel: (604) 922 8820.
**One Stitch at a Time**, Thistledown, 78 Main Street, PO Box 114, Picton, Ontario K0K 2T0. Tel: (613) 476 2453.
**Pointers Inc,** 1017 Mount Pleasant Road, Toronto, Ontario M4P 2M1.
Tel: (416) 322 9461.
Fax: (416) 488 8802.

## DMC RETAILERS
DMC embroidery threads are available in many retail outlets. Information on retailers in the US and Canada can be obtained from:
**DMC Corporation**, 10 Port Kearny, South Kearny, New Jersey 07032.
Tel: (201) 589 0606. Fax: (201) 589 8931.

**Author's acknowledgments**

The whole world owes a debt to William Morris and I am privileged and delighted to acknowledge mine. Without the legacy of his fabulous talents, this book could not have been written.

There is another person who contributed enormously to its development: my husband Peter. His knowledge of needlepoint and book production, together with his ability to understand both me and my scribbles, make him irreplaceable.

Without the family and friends who keep Designers Forum ticking over so efficiently and who give constant help and encouragement, there would be no time for books in my life. Particular thanks to Nick, Paul and Julie; Sam for her gentle editing; Sheila Thom for her delicious salads and impeccable stitching; Kate Hargreaves and Mog Fry for doing odd jobs with very even tempers; John Greenwood for his much admired brochure photography; Simon Deighton for printing our canvases so superbly; Peter Armitage and all at Appleton for their unbeatable colors and much appreciated efficiency; Robert and Phyllis Steed for their valued advice and marvelous drawings; Selina Winter for her calm kindness and both she and Angela Reader for the perfection of their stitching. The charts are works of art and once again I most sincerely thank Ethan Danielson; also on the subject of charts, my gratitude to

James Ohene-Djan for putting my first computerized efforts into print. And special thanks to Dorothy Vernon for making such lovely cushions and hangings so very quickly and expertly.

With imaginative styling by Cathy Sinker, the lovely photographs are by Jan Baldwin in some terrific locations – thanks to Leslie Harrington for finding them and for designing the book; and to Edward Hollamby at Red House, Jane Grundy and Barbara Twiss at Standen, Patrick Cooke at Athelhampton, Lord Saye and Sele at Broughton Castle, David and June Bowerman of Matfield, Kent, for allowing us to visit, and Amanda Hutchinson at Liberty of London for helping to arrange our photography in such a beautiful and appropriate store.

Beverley Byrne, with her great eye for Arts & Crafts furnishings, found the fire screen used for Vine; Rainer Steimann of Zweigart kindly sent the extra-wide canvas for the large Peacock hanging and the Flower Border rug; DMC generously supplied cotton embroidery thread; The Ladies' Work Society made up the Kelmscott Frame, and Greg Ross the footstool for the Acanthus & Flower, really beautifully. The research photographs are thanks to the tireless efforts of Claire Taylor; the editing to the patience and tact of Helen Ridge. Many thanks, too, to John Brandon-Jones for his helpful and interesting advice.

---

**Publisher's acknowledgments**

*The publisher thanks the following organizations for their kind permission to reproduce the photographs in this book:*
Jacket background: **The National Trust Photographic Library**/Andreas von Einsiedel
**Archiv für Kunst und Geschichte:** Royal Academy, London 17 (detail); **Bibliotheca Philosophic Hermetica,** Amsterdam 109; **Bodleian Library,** Oxford (MS. Auct. D. inf. 2. 11, fol. 7r) 31; **Bridgeman Art Library,** London: Aberdeen University Library 65/ Agnew & Sons, London 38/ Anthony Crane Collection 40/ Hessiches Landesmuseum, Darmstadt 12/ The Maas Gallery, London 49/ The De Morgan Foundation, London 70/ William Morris Gallery (London Borough of Waltham Forest) 39 (detail), 55, 57 (detail)/ Tate Gallery, London 92 (detail)/ Victoria & Albert Museum, London 7 above (detail), 15 below, 61 (detail), 63 (detail), 81, 93; **British Library,** London 25; **Kelmscott Manor** (The

Society of Antiquaries of London) 7 below (detail), 41, 101 (detail), 102 below; **Leighton House** (Royal Borough of Kensington & Chelsea) 18; **Museo dell' Opera della Metropolitana,** Siena: Fabio Lensini **105** (detail); **Courtesy of the National Portrait Gallery,** London 8 (detail); **The National Trust Photographic Library:** Mike Caldwell 84/ Andreas von Einsiedel 7 top (detail), 13; **The British Architectural Library, RIBA,** London 27; **Sanderson Design Archive** 77; **Victoria & Albert Museum,** London: 7 center (detail), 14–15, 71 (detail), 72–3, 75, 79, 102 above; **William Morris Gallery** (London Borough of Waltham Forest) 43, 83, 87 (detail), 89 (detail), 100, 103

*The publisher also thanks:* Harper & Tom's Flowers of London W11, Sally Harding, Helen Green, Alison Bolus, Danielle Gero, and Janet Smy.

**Index**

*Original Morris designs are given in italics.*

**A**

Acanthus & Flower design, 115
footstool, 115
*Acanthus and Vine* tapestry, 101-2
*African Marigold* fabric, 43
African Marigold design, 43
rug, 44-7
*Angeli Laudantes* tapestry, 61, 63
*Angeli Ministrantes* tapestry, 61
Apples design, 75-7
*Apples* wallpaper, 77
Appleton yarns, 17, 119
retailers, 124-5
*Art of the People*, 71
Arthur Sanderson & Sons, 79
*Artichoke*
embroidered panel, 17, 83, 87, 89
silk panels, 84
Artichoke design, 83-4
Artichoke I cushion, 86-7
Artichoke II cushion, 88-9
Arts & Crafts
Exhibition (1888), 55
fire screen, 79
Society, 61
Arts & Crafts Alphabet design, 67
Athelhampton, 16, 19

**B**

backing fabric, 122
basic techniques, 117-23

Beale, Margaret, 84
Beale family, 31, 77
Bees design, 55, 65
Blatchford, Robert, 103
book cover design, 113
bookmark designs, 109, 111
Book of Hours, 15, 17, 31
Broughton Castle, 25, 85, 116, 123
Brown, Ford Madox, 40, 73
Burden, Bessie, 83
Burden, Jane *see* Morris, Janey
Burne-Jones, Edward
angel designs, 61
at Oxford, 31, 39
at Red House, 40
at The Grange, 72
decorated books, 105, 115
The Firm, 73
Burne-Jones family home, 93
Burne-Jones, Georgiana, 83, 103
buttonhole thread, 33

**C**

*Cabbage and Vine* tapestry *see Acanthus and Vine*
canvas, 118
marking, 120
trimming, 122
chair seat, 81
charts, working from, 117-18
*Chaucer*, 100, 103
*Clarion, The*, 103
colors
background, 49, 55, 65, 75, 84
giving shape, 25, 27
sort in daylight, 18, 120

cord, splicing, 122
cotton floss, 119
Crane, Walter, 18
cushion designs, 27, 35, 53, 57, 63, 87, 89, 94, 95, 96

**D**

*Daisy* wallpaper, 93
*De Claris Mulieribus*, 105
De Morgan, William, 17, 25, 84, 101
Dearle, Henry, 15, 49, 61, 73, 75
Debenham, Lord, 17
designing with a computer, 94-5, 105
DMC cotton floss, 119
retailers, 125
dressing-room stool, 45

**E**

embossed letters, 67
embroidered panels, 83
embroidery, 40
free, 83, 113
Epping Forest, 14, 75
evening purse, 112

**F**

fabrics, evenweave, 118
Faulkner, Charles, 40, 83
finishing, 120
bookmarks, 123
chair seats and stools, 123
cushions, 122
fire screens, 123
hangings, 123
Kelmscott Frame, 123
rugs, 123
stools, 123
stretching, 122
fire screen designs, 18, 81
*Flora* tapestry, 61

Flower Border design, 49
cushion, 52-3
rug, 52-3
footstool, 114 15
*Forest, The*, tapestry 14-15, 17, 25, 27
watercolor, 27
frames, embroidery, 119
framing, 120
Frederick, Lord Leighton, 18
Freer Gallery of Art, 17
*Fruit* wallpaper design, 93, 97
Fruit design, 93-5
*see also* Lemon, Orange, Peach, Pomegranate

**G**

*Garden Tulip* wallpaper, 113
gauge, 118
Godman, Ada Phoebe, 83
gradual, Cathedral of Siena, 105
Grape design, 109
bookmark, 109

**H**

*Hauteloom* (High Loom) weaving technique, 14
Hestercombe House, 66-7
gardens, 61
Orangery, 42
Honeysuckle Border design, 55
cushion, 56-7, 65
*Honeysuckle* printed linen, 55
Horrington House, Turnham Green, 72

**I**

Ionides, Alexander, 14, 17

**J**

Jack, Annie, 84
Jeffrey & Co., 93
jewelry box, 27

**K**

Kelmscott Frame design, 94, 105-7
Kelmscott House, 14, 84, 93, 101-3
Kelmscott Manor, 40, 71-3, 93, 101, 103
Kelmscott Press, 61, 67, 79, 100, 103, 105, 109, 115

**L**

*La Belle Dame sans Merci* (painting), 12
Leek, Staffordshire, dyeing factory, 43
Leek School of Embroidery, 83
Leighton House, 18
Lemon design, 94
cushion, 94
workbox, 119
*Les Très Riches Heures du Duc de Berry*, 15
*Lesser Arts, The*, 101
Leyland, Lord, 17
Liberty of London, 43, 64-5, 104
Lion design, 31
cushion, 32-5

**M**

Marshall (one of The Firm), 40, 73
*Medway* fabric, 113
Merton Abbey, 14-15, 43, 55, 61, 75, 101-2, 113
*Message of the March Wind, The*, 13

**Places to visit**

*Standen*, East Grinstead, West Sussex (National Trust) – for the Webb house, garden, woods and the Morris & Co. furnishings.
*Wightwick Manor*, Wolverhampton, West Midlands (National Trust) – for the collection of Morris furnishings and the garden.
*Red House*, Bexleyheath, Kent (Private – by appointment) – for Morris and Janey's first home and Webb's architecture.
*Kelmscott Manor*, Lechlade, Oxfordshire (Society of Antiquaries) – for the sixteenth-century house and collection of Morris hangings and furniture.
*Kelmscott House*, Hammersmith, London – for the Kelmscott printing press and headquarters of the William Morris Society (membership details from 26 Upper Mall, Hammersmith, London W6 9TA).
*Liberty*, Regent Street, London – frequently visited by Morris and his Pre-Raphaelite friends, it has retained its original charm. As well as displaying and selling a wide range of my needlepoint kits, it has an exceptional Arts & Crafts furnishings department.
*Victoria & Albert Museum*, South Kensington, London
*William Morris Gallery*, Walthamstow, London
*Fitzwilliam Museum*, Cambridge
There are many other places with Morris connections and exhibits: Bedford: *Cecil Higgins Museum*. Birmingham: *City Museum and Art Gallery*. Bristol: *Museum and Art Gallery*. Cambridge: *Jesus College*; *Queen's College*. Cheltenham: *Art Gallery & Museum*. Leicester: *County Museum and Art Gallery*. London: *Leighton House*, Kensington; *Linley Sambourne House*, Kensington. Manchester: *Whitworth Art Gallery*. Norwich: *Castle Museum*. Oxford: *Oxford Union*. Uxbridge: *Arthur Sanderson & Sons (Archive)*.

**Bibliography**

It is hardly surprising that many books have been written about the life and works of such a multitalented man. My favorites are:
*William Morris, A Life for Our Time* (Fiona MacCarthy, Faber and Faber, 1994)
*William Morris Decor and Design* (Elizabeth Wilhide, Pavilion, 1991)
*The Art of William Morris* (Aymer Vallance, Dover, 1990)
*William Morris* (Helen Dore, Pyramid Books, 1990)
*William Morris, His Life and Work* (Stephen Coote, Garamond, 1990)
*William Morris* (Christine Poulson, Apple Press, 1989)
*William Morris and the Arts and Crafts Movement* (Linda Parry, Studio Editions, 1989)
*Textiles of the Arts and Crafts Movement* (Linda Parry, Thames and Hudson, 1988)
*William Morris by Himself* (Gillian Naylor, Macdonald Orbis, 1988)
*William Morris Designs and Patterns* (Norah Gillow, Bracken Books, 1988)
*The Life and Work of William Morris* (Aymer Vallance, 1897; republished Studio Editions, 1986)
*William Morris Textiles* (Linda Parry, Weidenfeld & Nicolson, 1983)
*Textiles by William Morris and Morris & Co., 1861-1940* (Oliver Fairclough & Emmeline Leary, Thames and Hudson, 1981)
*The Arts and Crafts Movement* (Gillian Naylor, Studio Vista, 1980)
*William Morris Wallpapers & Chintzes* (Fiona Clark, St Martin's Press/Academy Editions, 1973)
*William Morris as Designer* (Ray Watkinson, Studio Vista, 1967)
A catalog by Linda Parry will be published in Spring 1996 to accompany the William Morris centenary exhibition at the Victoria & Albert Museum, London (May-September 1996).